OF TRUE RELIGION

ST. AUGUSTINE

Of True Religion

Introduction by Louis O. Mink
Translated by J. H. S. Burleigh

A Gateway Edition

REGNERY/GATEWAY, INC.

SOUTH BEND, INDIANA

First published 1953 by the Westminster Press, Philadelphia, and by the S.C.M. Press Ltd., London.

Introduction copyright © 1959 by Regnery/Gateway, Inc., 120 West LaSalle Avenue, South Bend, Indiana 46601. Manufactured in the United States of America, 2–79.

ISBN: 0-89526-926-0

CONTENTS

INTRODUCTION

Framing the turbulent centuries in which the empire of the Eternal City perished and the history of the West became the history of Christendom stand two men who left personal records of their search for understanding in a chaotic world. As chance would have it, both were named Aurelius. Marcus Aurelius, the great Stoic emperor of the second century, summed up in his *Meditations* the values which had created but could not save the last flowering of the classical world. Little more than two centuries later, Aurelius Augustinus was converted to the church, now powerful and expanding, which Marcus Aurelius had persecuted as a sect on the fanatic fringe. As Augustine lay dying in 430 A.D., Rome had long since become another provincial city, and the Vandals were beginning a successful siege of his episcopal city of Hippo in North Africa. But Augustine, who began his career as a professor of literature and ended it as the bishop of a then great city, did more than his namesake the emperor to salvage something from the ruins of the Greek and Roman world. In the alembic of his inquiring mind, a classical tradition stemming from Plato was fused with Christian doctrine to produce a complex of ideas which shaped medieval thought for a millennium to come. There is a story that Charlemagne had Augustine's works read aloud to him to occupy his mind; and Martin Luther was of course an Augustinian monk. Both the Holy Roman Emperor and the founder of Protestantism stand in the shadow he cast along the centuries. But a great German historian has also called him the "first modern man," referring to his preoccupation with the analysis of subjective experience and individual personality.

The Augustine we are likely to know today is the Augustine who, already a bishop, wrote two very different books: the *Confessions*, which was the first autobiography, and the *City of God*, which was the first philosophy of history. The *Confessions* is an intimate record of Augustine's spiritual journey, vivid in detail and personal in scale. In the form of an extended prayer (Marcus Aurelius's *Meditations* were addressed to himself), its chief theme is Augustine's clinical dissection of his motives and beliefs in the years before the momentous event of his conversion to Christianity. The *City of God*, on the other hand, is an enormous and rambling work, written over a period of thirteen years and finished only a few years before Augustine's death. It was begun as an answer to the charge that Christianity had led to the decay of the Roman Empire by weakening its institutions and morale. But it grew eventually into an extended history of two "cities": the City of the World and the invisible City of

God. One might wonder how the same mind could be as introspective and psychologically subtle as in the *Confessions*, and so encyclopedic and panoramic as in the *City of God*. Yet Augustine was at the same time the "prophet of personality," as Edwyn Bevan called him, and the architect of a vision of universal history in which the rise and fall of empires are seen as the massive work of God's providence. This preoccupation both with the depths and nuances of inner experience and with the sweep of all history and nature is the riddle of Augustine, and the clue to its solution is more easily to be found in his earlier than in his later works. When Augustine became a bishop in 396 A.D., his duty of sustaining the faith and confounding heretics and schismatics occasioned the long series of books and tracts which define what is commonly called Augustinianism. In most of these, Augustine was working out the logic of orthodox belief in his refutation of errors. Against the Donatists, who claimed independence from the church, he defended the unity and authority of the single catholic church. Against the Manicheans, who held that a principle of evil in the world limits God's power, he argued that God's omnipotence and goodness make impossible the existence of genuine evil. Against the Pelagians, who believed that men could merit salvation through effort and moral purpose, he gave uncommon emphasis to the doctrine of original sin and the arbitrariness of grace, freely granted by God to some men and withheld from others although merited by none. His theological works are so polemical, in fact, and their influence has been so great, that it is possible to lose Augustine in Augustinianism and to miss the inquiring mind behind the dogmatic theology. Augustine himself became the "doctor of grace" only after a long and difficult intellectual journey. He had himself believed, with the fervor he always displayed, many of the views which he later refuted. He had believed them because they answered his questions, for a time, and his conversion to Christianity meant not an abandonment of the questions but the discovery of a better answer.

In the five years between his conversion in 386 and his ordination as a priest in 391, Augustine spent much of his time living in monastic seclusion with groups of friends, engaged in meditation, discussion and writing. Some of the treatises of this period are so exclusively philosophical that it has been argued that it was to neo-platonism rather than to Christianity that he had been converted. But this can hardly be said of his essay "Of True Religion," which is very possibly the last treatise which he wrote as a layman. He sent it in 390 to Romanianus, an elder friend who had helped to finance his education, had later followed him into Manicheanism, and whom he was now trying to convert to Christianity. Coming, as it does, at the mid-point of his life, this essay represents the climax of Augustine's philosophical odyssey, and the beginning of his theological career. Perhaps nowhere else can one see so clearly the interpenetration of philosophy and theology which illustrates his famous dictum *Credo, ut intelligam:* I believe, in order that I may understand. Since its ostensible argument is that Christianity is the truth which philosophers have sought and dimly anticipated, it might almost be called "Of True Philosophy." But Augustine would have seen no difference.

Most of the arguments which Augustine addresses to the reader in this essay are the arguments by which he had convinced himself. At the age of nineteen, he had been converted from popular paganism to Manicheanism, and had remained a devout (and highly voluble) Manichean for nine years. Founded in the third century A.D., Manicheanism was by Augustine's time a religious system rivaling Christianity. At the heart of Manicheanism was a dramatic and spectacular myth: at the beginning of the world there were two substances, light and darkness, or the kingdom of good and the kingdom of evil. Each kingdom was elaborately organized into hierarchies and orders. The great sweep of cosmic history is the warfare between these two kingdoms, with the Princes of Darkness seeking to swallow and imprison portions of light, and the Angels of

Light seeking to liberate imprisoned light and to drive the forces of darkness back to their own territorial limits. The world of nature and the human soul are the arenas where this conflict is carried on: an eclipse, for instance, is a temporary victory for darkness, shortly beaten back in a counterattack by light. Similarly, the passion of avarice or lust is a victory, rather less temporary, for darkness against light. Man himself is not a combatant but merely a battlefield in this world war.

Presumably it was not the elaborate ritual or baroque mythology of Manicheanism that appealed to Augustine, but the high standards of morality it enjoined, and most of all the philosophical basis which gave it a kind of explanatory power. (As Augustine says, Manicheanism gave him the pleasure of winning many debates with ignorant Christians.) For one thing, Manicheanism recognized no reality which was not visible or tangible, that is, material. Light and darkness, good and evil, "spirit" and "matter" were alike for it physical entities occupying space-time, and nothing was real which could not be pictured in a visible model. It was also radically dualistic. Good and evil (that is, light and darkness), it taught, were equally primeval. They could displace but not destroy each other. Man is the victim, not the author of the evil he does.

On both of these points, Manicheanism has a certain intellectual appeal which has helped the name to survive as a type of thought long after the religious system of Manicheanism disappeared (in part through Augustine's efforts). Both its materialism and its dualism provide a single pattern of explanation for natural and human events. And its doctrine of radical and uncreated evil gives intellectual expression to a variety of moods and experiences in which the forces of nature and the springs of human action seem irredeemably destructive on a vast scale.

But Augustine's doubts about Manicheanism grew, and became critical when in Rome he discovered that the sceptics who called themselves "Academics" had constructed an entire philosophy of doubt—much older, in fact, than either Manicheanism or Christianity. Knowledge is possible, the academics taught, neither through the senses nor through the understanding: not through the senses, because the objects of sense are in constant change and the senses themselves deceptive; not through the understanding, because equally good arguments can be given on both sides of an issue. Probability must suffice in place of certainty, the Academics counselled, and fallible judgment in place of knowledge. Although this could not satisfy Augustine for long, the critical techniques which supported scepticism made Manicheanism seem thin and fantastic.

The Academics were remote heirs of Plato's philosophy, as the Academy was the remote

descendant of the school founded by him. But
Plato's philosophy had two sides: scepticism
about knowledge of the experienced world,
and confidence in the possibility of knowledge
of an intelligible realm of ideas accessible only
to reason. Augustine probably never realized
that in passing with his usual enthusiasm from
scepticism to neo-platonism he was turning
from one Platonic inheritance to another. In
neo-platonism (which Augustine knew as
"Platonism"), he found at last an intellectual
system which could satisfy at once his need for
certainty and his capacity for criticism. Almost
singlehandedly he converted it into a Christian
philosophy. Later he attacked neo-platonism
as he attacked other heresies and errors, but he
held the "Platonists" superior to all other philosophers nevertheless.

What made neo-platonism uniquely appropriate to a Christian interpretation was its conception of the absolute unity, transcendence
and reality of God, whom Plotinus (whose
Enneads Augustine read in Latin translation)
could speak of only as the ineffable *One*. From
the One, according to the neo-platonists,
comes to be by a series of "emanations," or
overflows of being, all the diversity of the spiritual and physical worlds: first, universal Mind
and its objects, the truths of mathematics and
physics known by reason alone; second, universal Soul, the source and creator of life; then,
in a continuing series of emanations, the whole

scale of intelligent, animate and inanimate nature. The scale of being becomes at each remove from the One less unified and coherent, less intelligible, and more "material." But every level retains a spark of divine being inherited from the primal source. Man lies midway in the scale of being, capable of rising higher in the level of Mind (or even higher in mystical experience) or of falling to the level of mere body.

In this religio-philosophical system, Augustine found the suggestion of answers to the questions which had endured through his successive intellectual conversions. The insistent presence of evil in the world is interpreted, not as an entity or power belonging to things, but as a measure of their distance from the source of their being. As Augustine insists throughout *Of True Religion*, all existence is good, and nothing is evil in itself. A human choice may become evil, not as such or because its object is evil, but because it substitutes a lower for a higher possible good.

Neo-platonism also provided for Augustine an alternative to Manichean materialism by its conception of degrees of reality which can be known to reason but not sensed or imagined. Neither for neo-platonism nor for Augustine could the primal source of being be known even by reason: "God is not offered to the corporeal senses, and transcends even the mind." But as the visible world witnesses to the existence of an invisible but intelligible world, so the latter witnesses to its ground and creator. There is nothing anthropomorphic about Augustine's idea of God. God is neither imaginable nor conceivable, but is the ground and condition of all existence and knowledge. There is nothing remarkable, Augustine thinks, in knowing that seven plus five is twelve (as one can tell by counting) or that two windows in a wall are aesthetically more pleasing if they are the same size (as one can tell by looking). But there is something very remarkable in the fact that we can see that seven plus five not only is but *must* be twelve, and that the arrangement of forms not only does but *must* obey laws of order and symmetry. We could not distinguish between what a sum happens to be and what it necessarily must be, Augustine believes (like Plato before him), if there were not absolute standards of truth and of beauty "higher than the mind."

So Augustine answers at once the Manicheans and the sceptics. Against the latter he argues that one could not even recognize an error unless one has a standard of truth; and, moreover, even if the sceptic were to doubt everything, he could not doubt that he was doubting, and hence would be certain of the truth that he doubts. (More than a thousand years later, this argument became, as Descartes' "I think, therefore I am," a starting point of "modern" philosophy.) And against the Manicheans, Augustine argues that knowledge of the material world presupposes knowledge of truths not learned from experience, and testifying to a spiritual world.

Augustine's essay on "true religion" sounds to modern ears more like an exhortation than like an argument. In part this is due to the fact that Augustine was one of the most learned rhetoricians of his time, and applied with great skill rules of style which regarded step-by-step argument as dull and graceless, and sought to interest and to persuade by excursions, interludes and repetitions. But the essay incorporates the thrust of argument which is peculiarly Augustine's. It begins with experience: we cannot, he agrees with the sceptics, reach certain truth about the world of things seen, touched and heard. But this very uncertainty leads to philosophy as a second step; thought discovers its own truths and standards, and recognizes in them a necessity and unity which is not its own. "Do not go abroad. Return within yourself. In the inward man dwells truth. If you find that you are by nature mutable, transcend yourself. But remember in doing so that you must also transcend yourself even as a reasoning soul. Make for the place where the light of reason is kindled." So the final step for Augustine is religion: the recognition that the truth of the mind's ideas is grounded in God, who is the creator of mind and its objects and who illuminates the mind to make it capable of knowledge. The direction of thought, as Etienne Gilson has pointed out, is from external things to interior experience, and from interior experience to superior reality.

Now this is at the same time an argument and an autobiography. It is an attempt to convince, but it is also an expression of Augustine's personal experience, and it is not a simple matter to disentangle the cogency of his thought from the intensity of his experience. Nowhere better than in this essay can one see the extent to which Augustine regards intellectual understanding as something vividly and intensely alive rather than coldly and mechanically objective. He demands rational answers to real questions, but also that the answers be personally possessed as well as logically adequate. Truth must be willed as well as thought. In this respect Augustine differs greatly from both Plato and Descartes, between whom he is in many ways a bridge. Plato thought of the will as an automatic corollary of reason, and Descartes thought of the will as reason's antagonist. But for Augustine, reason and will are conditions of each other and inseparable from each other.

Perhaps this is the key to the problem of Augustine's combination of subtle psychological introspection with a panoramic view of universal history. For an age which has sharply distinguished the subjective from the objective the problem has been to get them back together again. But for Augustine they have a common ground and a single Creator, and hence a conformity with each other which we do not have to discover because it is where we begin. As he says in the *Confessions* (X,vi,10): "If a man merely stares at the world, while another not only sees but questions it, the world does not appear differently to them; but appearing the same to both, it is dumb to one and answers the other. Or rather it speaks to all, but only those can understand it who compare its answer with the truth that is within them."

Louis O. Mink

Of True Religion

THE TEXT

i, 1. The way of the good and blessed life is to be found entirely in the true religion wherein one God is worshipped and acknowledged with purest piety to be the beginning of all existing things, originating, perfecting and containing the universe. Thus it becomes easy to detect the error of the peoples who have preferred to worship many gods rather than the true God and Lord of all things, because their wise men whom they call philosophers used to have schools in disagreement one with another, while all made common use of the temples. The peoples and the priests knew quite well how divergent were the views of the philosophers concerning the nature of the gods, for none shrank from publicly professing his opinion, and indeed each endeavoured as far as he could to persuade everybody. And yet all of them with their co-sectaries, in spite of their diverse and mutually hostile opinions, came to the common religious rites, none saying them nay. Now the question is not, Whose opinion was nearest to the truth? But one thing, so far as I can see, is abundantly clear. What the philosophers observed along with the people in the way of religious rites was something quite different from what they defended in private, or even in the hearing of the people.

ii, 2. Socrates is said to have been somewhat bolder than the others. He swore by a dog or a stone or any other object that happened to be near him or came to hand, so to speak, when he was to take an oath. I suppose he knew how many natural objects, produced and governed by divine providence, are much better than the works of human artificers, and therefore worthier of divine honours than are the images which are worshipped in the temples. Not that dogs and stones were rightly to be worshipped by wise men; but that in this way all who had intelligence might understand how sunk in superstition men are. He wanted to show that an oath of this kind did represent an advance though not a very great one. If men were ashamed to take this step, they might at least see how shameful it was to remain in the still baser condition of religious practice to which they were accustomed. At the same time those who supposed that the visible world was the supreme God were given to realize their turpitude, for they were taught that any stone might be rightly worshipped as a particle of God most high. If they saw that that was offensive, they might change their minds and seek the one God who alone is superior to our minds, and by whom clearly every soul and the whole world has been created. Plato afterwards wrote all this down, making it pleasant to read rather than potent to persuade. These men were not fit to change the minds of their fellow-citizens, and convert them from idolatrous superstition and worldly vanity to the true worship of the true God. Thus Socrates himself venerated images along with his people, and after his condemnation and death no one dared to swear by a dog or to call a stone Jupiter. These things were merely recorded and handed down to memory. Whether this was due to fear of punishment or to the influence of the times it is not for me to judge.

iii, 3. This, however, I will say with complete confidence, in spite of all who love so obstinately the books of the philosophers. In Christian times there can be no doubt at all as to which religion is to be received and held fast, and as to where is the way that leads to truth and beatitude. Suppose Plato were alive and would not spurn a question I would put to him; or rather suppose one of his own disciples, who lived at the same time as he did, had addressed him thus: "You have persuaded me that truth is seen not with the bodily eyes but by the pure mind, and that any soul that cleaves to truth is thereby made happy and perfect. Nothing hinders the perception of truth more than a life devoted to lusts, and the false images of sensible things, derived from the sensible world and impressed on us by the agency of the body, which beget various opinions and errors. Therefore the mind has to be healed so that it may behold the immutable form of things which remains ever the same, preserving its beauty unchanged and unchangeable, knowing no spatial distance or temporal variation, abiding absolutely one and the same. Men do not believe in its existence, though it alone truly and supremely exists. Other things are born, die, are dissolved or broken up. But so far as they do exist they have existence from the eternal God, being created by his truth. To the rational and intellectual soul is given to enjoy the contemplation of his eternity, and by that contemplation it is armed and equipped so that it may obtain eternal life. So long as it is weakened by love of things that come to be and pass away, or by pain at losing them, so long as it is devoted to the custom of this life and to the bodily senses, and becomes vain among vain images, it laughs at those who say that there is something which cannot be seen by the eyes, or conjured up by any phantasm, but can be beheld by the mind alone, by the intelligence. You, my master, have persuaded me to believe these things. Now, if some great and divine man should arise to persuade the peoples that such things were to be at least believed if they could not grasp them with the mind, or that those who could grasp them should not allow themselves to be implicated in the depraved opinions of the multitude or to be overborne by vulgar errors, would you not

judge that such a man is worthy of divine honours?" I believe Plato's answer would be:
"That could not be done by man, unless the
very virtue and wisdom of God delivered him
from natural environment, illumined him
from his cradle not by human teaching but by
personal illumination, honoured him with such
grace, strengthened him with such firmness and
exalted him with such majesty, that he should
be able to despise all that wicked men desire,
to suffer all that they dread, to do all that they
marvel at, and so with the greatest love and
authority to convert the human race to so
sound a faith. But it is needless to ask me about
the honours that would be due to such a man.
It is easy to calculate what honours are due to
the wisdom of God. Being the bearer and in-
strument of the wisdom of God on behalf of
the true salvation of the human race, such a
man would have earned a place all his own, a
place above all humanity."

4. Now this very thing has come to pass. It
is celebrated in books and documents. From
one particular region of the earth in which
alone the one God was worshipped and where
alone such a man could be born, chosen men
were sent throughout the entire world, and by
their virtues and words have kindled the fires
of the divine love. Their sound teaching has
been confirmed and they have left to posterity
a world illumined. But not to speak of ancient
history, which anyone may refuse to believe,

today throughout the nations and peoples the proclamation is made: "In the beginning was the Word, and the Word was with God, and the Word was God. This was in the beginning with God, and all things were made by him, and without him was nothing made" (John 1:1). In order that men may receive the Word, love him, and enjoy him so that the soul may be healed and the eye of the mind receive power to use the light, to the greedy it is declared: "Lay not up for yourselves treasures upon earth where moth and rust destroy, and where thieves break through and steal. But lay up for yourselves treasures in heaven where neither moth nor rust destroys, and where thieves do not break through nor steal. For where your treasure is there will your heart be also" (Matt. 6:19). To the wanton it is said: "He who sows in the flesh shall of the flesh reap corruption. He who sows in the spirit shall of the spirit reap eternal life" (Gal. 6:8). To the proud it is said: "Whosoever exalteth himself shall be abased and whosoever humbleth himself shall be exalted" (Luke 14:11). To the wrathful it is said: "Thou has received a blow. Turn the other cheek" (Matt. 5:39). To those who strive it is said: "Love your enemies" (Matt. 5:44). To the superstitious: "The kingdom of God is within you" (Luke 17:21). To the curious: "Look not on the things which are seen, but on the things which are not seen. For the things which are seen are temporal,

but the things which are not seen are eternal"
(II Cor. 4:18). Finally, to all it is said: "Love
not the world nor the things which are in the
world. For everything that is in the world is
the lust of the flesh, the lust of the eyes and the
ambition of this world" (I John 2:15).

5. These things are read to the peoples
throughout all the earth and are listened to
most gladly and with veneration. After all the
Christian blood shed, after all the burnings and
crucifixions of the martyrs, fertilized by these
things churches have sprung up as far afield as
among barbarian nations. That thousands of
young men and maidens contemn marriage
and live in chastity causes no one surprise.
Plato might have suggested that, but he so
dreaded the perverse opinion of his times that
he is said to have given in to nature and declared continence to be no sin. Views are accepted which it was once monstrous to maintain, even as it is monstrous now to dispute
them. All over the inhabited world the Christian rites are entrusted to men who are willing
to make profession and to undertake the obli-
gations required. Every day the precepts of
Christianity are read in the churches and expounded by the priests. Those who try to ful-
fil them beat their breasts in contrition. Multitudes enter upon this way of life from every
race, forsaking the riches and honours of the
present world, desirous of dedicating their
whole life to the one most high God. Islands

once deserted and many lands formerly left in solitude are filled with monks. In cities and towns, castles and villages, country places and private estates, there is openly preached and practised such a renunciation of earthly things and conversion to the one true God that daily throughout the entire world with almost one voice the human race makes response: Lift up your hearts to the Lord. Why, then, do we still admiringly yearn for the darkness of yesterday, and look for divine oracles in the entrails of dead cattle? Why, when it comes to disputation, are we so eager to mouth the name of Plato rather than to have the truth in our hearts?

iv, 6. Those who think it a vain or even a wicked thing to despise the world of sense, and to subject the soul to God most high that he may purge it with virtue, must be refuted with a different argument; if indeed they are worth disputing with. But those who admit that that is a good ideal to be pursued should acknowledge God and submit to him who has brought it to pass that all nations now are persuaded that these things ought to be believed. They would themselves have brought this to pass if they had had the power. Seeing they had not the power, they cannot avoid the charge of envy. Let them, then, submit to him who has brought it to pass. Let them not be prevented by inquisitiveness or by vain-glory from recognizing the gap that subsists between the timid guesses of the few and the obvious salvation and correction of whole peoples. If Plato and the rest of them, in whose names men glory, were to come to life again and find the churches full and the temples empty, and that the human race was being called away from desire for temporal and transient goods to spiritual and intelligible goods and to the hope of eternal life, and was actually giving its attention to these things, they would perhaps say (if they really were the men they are said to have been): That is what we did not dare to preach to the people. We preferred to yield to popular custom rather than to bring the people over to our way of thinking and living.

7. So if these men could live their lives again today, they would see by whose authority measures are best taken for man's salvation, and, with the change of a few words and sentiments, they would become Christians, as many Platonists of recent times have done. If they would not admit this or do this, but remained in their pride and envy, I know not whether it would be possible for them, encumbered with these rags and bird-lime, to resort to the things they once said were to be sought and striven for. I do not know whether such great men would have been prevented by the other vice which prevents present-day pagans, who now concern us, from accepting the Christian salvation, for indeed it is utterly puerile. I mean, of course, their curiosity in inquiring at demons.

v, 8. However philosophers may boast, any-one can easily understand that religion is not to be sought from them. For they take part in the religious rites of their fellow-citizens, but in their schools teach divergent and contrary opinions about the nature of their gods and of the chief good, as the multitude can testify. If we could see this one great vice healed by the Christian discipline, no one should deny that that would be an achievement worthy of all possible praise. Innumerable heresies that turn aside from the rule of Christianity testify that men are not admitted to sacramental commun-ion who think and endeavour to persuade others to think otherwise of God the Father, of his wisdom and of the divine gift [the Holy Spirit] than as the truth demands. So it is taught and believed as a chief point in man's salvation that philosophy, i.e., the pursuit of wisdom, cannot be quite divorced from relig-ion, for those whose doctrine we do not ap-prove do not share in *our* sacramental rites.

9. There is little to be surprised at in this in the case of men who have chosen to have dif-ferent religious rites from ours such as the Ophites whoever they may be, or the Mani-cheans and others. It is more noticeable in the case of those who celebrate similar religious rites but differ from us in doctrine and are more vigorous in defending their errors than careful to have them corrected. These are ex-cluded from Catholic communion and from

participation in our rites in spite of their similarity. They have deserved to have names of their own and separate meetings, being different not only in matters of words, but also because of their superstition; like the Photinians, the Arians and many others. It is another matter with those who have caused schisms. The Lord's threshing-floor might have kept them as chaff until the time of the last winnowing, had they not in their levity been carried off by the wind of pride, and separated from us of their own accord. The Jews, it is true, worship the one omnipotent God, but they expect from him only temporal and visible goods. Being too secure they were unwilling to observe in their own Scriptures the indications of a new people of God arising out of humble estate, and so they remained in "the old man." This being so, religion is to be sought neither in the confusion of the pagans, nor in the offscourings of the heretics, nor in the insipidity of schismatics, nor in the blindness of the Jews, but only among those who are called Catholic or orthodox Christians, that is, guardians of truth and followers of right.

vi, 10. This Catholic Church, strongly and widely spread throughout the world, makes use of all who err, to correct them if they are willing to be aroused, and to assist its own progress. It makes use of the nations as material for its operations, of heretics to try its own doctrine, of schismatics to prove its stability,

of the Jews as a foil to its own beauty. Some it
invites, others it excludes, some it leaves behind, others it leads. To all it gives power to
participate in the grace of God, whether they
are as yet to be formed or reformed, admitted
for the first time or gathered in anew. Its own
carnal members, i.e., those whose lives or opinions are carnal, it tolerates as chaff by which
the corn is protected on the floor until it is separated from its covering. On this floor everyone voluntarily makes himself either corn or
chaff. Therefore every man's sin or error is
tolerated until he finds an accuser or defends
his wicked opinion with pertinacious animosity. Those who are excluded return by way of
penitence, or in baleful liberty sink into wickedness as a warning to us to be diligent; or they
cause schisms to exercise our patience; or they
beget a heresy to try our intelligence or to
quicken it. By such ways carnal Christians
leave us, for they could neither be corrected
nor endured.

11. Often, too, divine providence permits
even good men to be driven from the congre-
gation of Christ by the turbulent seditions of
carnal men. When for the sake of the peace of
the Church they patiently endure that insult or
injury, and attempt no novelties in the way of
heresy or schism, they will teach men how
God is to be served with a true disposition and
with great and sincere charity. The intention
of such men is to return when the tumult has

subsided. But if that is not permitted because
the storm continues or because a fiercer one
might be stirred up by their return, they hold
fast to their purpose to look to the good even
of those responsible for the tumults and com-
motions that drove them out. They form no
separate conventicles of their own, but defend
to the death and assist by their testimony the
faith which they know is preached in the Catholic Church. These the Father who seeth in
secret crowns secretly. It appears that this is a
rare kind of Christian, but examples are not
lacking. Indeed there are more than can be believed. So divine providence uses all kinds of
men as examples for the oversight of souls and
for the building up of his spiritual people.

vii, 12. A few years ago, my dear Romanianus, I promised to write down for you my
sentiments concerning true religion. I think
the time has now come to do so. In view of the
love wherewith I am bound to you I can no
longer allow your eager questions to run on
endlessly. Repudiating all who do not carry
philosophy into religious observance or phi-
losophize in a religious spirit; those also who
wax proud in wicked opinions or some other
cause of dissension and so deviate from the
Rule of Faith and from the communion of the
Catholic Church; and those who refuse to own
the light of the Holy Scripture and the grace
of the spiritual people of God, which we call
the New Testament—all of whom I have cen-

sured as briefly as I could—we must hold fast
the Christian religion and the communion of
the Church which is Catholic, and is called
Catholic not only by its own members but
also by all its enemies. Whether they will or
no, heretics and schismatics use no other name
for it than the name of Catholic, when they
speak of it not among themselves but with
outsiders. They cannot make themselves understood unless they designate it by this name
which is in universal use.

13. In following this religion our chief concern is with the prophetic history of the dispensation of divine providence in time—what
God has done for the salvation of the human
race, renewing and restoring it unto eternal
life. When once this is believed, a way of life
agreeable to the divine commandments will
purge the mind and make it fit to perceive spiritual things which are neither past nor future
but abide ever the same, liable to no change.
There is one God; Father, Son and Holy
Spirit. When this Trinity is known as far as it
can be in this life, it is perceived without the
slightest doubt that every creature, intellectual, animal and corporeal, derives such existence as it has from that same creative Trinity,
has its own form, and is subject to the most
perfect order. It is not as if the Father were
understood to have made one part of creation,
the Son another, and the Holy Spirit another,
but the Father through the Son in the gift of

the Holy Spirit together made all things and every particular thing. For every thing, substance, essence or nature, or whatever better word there may be, possesses at once these three qualities: it is a particular thing; it is distinguished from other things by its own proper form; and it does not transgress the order of nature.

viii, 14. When this is known it will be as clear as it can be to m n that all things are subject by necessary, indefeasible and just laws to their Lord God. Hence all those things which to begin with we simply believed, following authority only, we come to understand. Partly we see them as certain, partly as possible and fitting, and we become sorry for those who do not believe them, and have preferred to mock at us for believing rather than to share our belief. The Holy Incarnation, the birth from a virgin, the death of the Son of God for us, his resurrection from the dead, ascension into heaven and sitting at the right hand of the Father, the forgiveness of sins, the day of judgment, the resurrection of the body are not merely believed, when the eternity of the Trinity and the mut bility of created things are known. They are also judged to be part and parcel of the mercy of the most high God, which he has shown towards the human race.

15. It has been truly said: "There must be many heresies, that they which are approved may be made manifest among you" (I Cor.

11:19). Let us also make use of that gift of divine providence. Men become heretics who would have no less held wrong opinions even within the Church. Now that they are outside they do us more good, not by teaching the truth, for they do not know it, but by provoking carnal Catholics to seek the truth and spiritual Catholics to expound it. There are in the Holy Church innumerable men approved by God, but they do not become manifest among us so long as we are delighted with the darkness of our ignorance, and prefer to sleep rather than to behold the light of truth. So, many are awakened from sleep by the heretics, so that they may see God's light and be glad. Let us therefore use even heretics, not to approve their errors, but to assert the Catholic discipline against their wiles, and to become more vigilant and cautious, even if we cannot recall them to salvation.

ix, 16. I believe that God will lend us his aid so that Scripture, being read by good men inspired by piety, may avail not against one false and bad opinion only but against all. But chiefly it is set against those who think that there are two natures or substances at war with one another, each with its own principle. Some things they like and others they dislike, and they will have God to be the author of the things they like, but not of those they dislike. When they cannot overcome temptation and are snared in carnal traps, they think there are two souls in one body, one from God and sharing his nature, the other from the race of darkness which God neither begat, nor made, nor produced, nor cast from him; which has its own independent life, its territory, its offspring and living things, in short its kingdom and unbegotten principle. At a certain time it rebelled against God, and God, having no other resource and finding no other means of resisting the enemy, under dire necessity, sent the good soul hither, a particle of his substance. They fondly imagine that the enemy was subdued and the world fabricated by this soul becoming mixed up with the elements of darkness.

17. I am not now refuting their opinions, partly because I have already done so and partly because I intend to do so again, if God permit. In this work I am showing as far as I can with the arguments God deigns to supply, how secure the Catholic faith is against them, and how the things which move men to give in to their opinions need not disturb the mind. You know my mind very well, and I want you above all to believe firmly that I do not make this solemn declaration with an arrogance which ought to be avoided. I say, whatever error is to be found in this book it alone is to be attributed to me. Whatever is truly and suitably expounded I owe entirely to God, the giver of all good gifts.

x, 18. Let it be clearly understood that there

could have been no error in religion had not
the soul worshipped in place of its God either
a soul or a body or some phantasm of its own,
possibly two of these together or all of them
at once. In this life the soul should have
frankly accepted the temporal condition of
human society but should have directed its regard to eternal things and worshipped the one
God without whose changeless permanence
no mutable thing could have any abiding existence. Anyone who studies his own emotions
can learn that the soul is mutable, not in space
certainly but in time. That body is mutable
both in space and time is easy for anyone to
observe. Phantasms are nothing but figments
of corporeal shapes appearing to bodily sense.
It is the easiest thing in the world to commit
them to memory as they appear or, by thinking about them, to divide or multiply, contract
or expand, set in order or disturb, or give them
any kind of shape. But when truth is being
sought it is difficult to be on one's guard against
them and to avoid them.

19. Do not, then, let us serve the creature
rather than the Creator, or become vain in our
thoughts. That is the rule of perfect religion.
If we cleave to the eternal Creator we must
necessarily be somehow affected by eternity.
But because the soul, implicated in and over-
whelmed by its sins, cannot by itself see and
grasp this truth, if in human experience there

were no intermediate stage whereby man
might strive to rise above his earthly life and
reach likeness to God, God in his ineffable
mercy by a temporal dispensation has used the
mutable creation, obedient however to his
eternal laws, to remind the soul of its original
and perfect nature, and so has come to the aid
of individual men and indeed of the whole human race. That is the Christian religion in our
times. To know and follow it is the most secure and most certain way of salvation.

20. This religion can be defended against
loquacious persons and expounded to seekers in
many ways. Omnipotent God may himself
show the truth, or he may use good angels or
men to assist men of good will to behold and
grasp the truth. Everyone uses the method
which he sees to be suitable to those with
whom he has to do. I have given much consideration for a long time to the nature of the
people I have met with either as carping critics
or as genuine seekers of the truth. I have also
considered my own case both when I was a
critic and when I was a seeker; and I have come
to the conclusion that this is the method I must
use. Hold fast whatever truth you have been
able to grasp, and attribute it to the Catholic
Church. Reject what is false and pardon me
who am but a man. What is doubtful believe
until either reason teaches or authority lays
down that it is to be rejected or that it is true,

or that it has to be believed always. Listen to
what follows as diligently and as piously as
you can. For God helps men like that.

xi, 21. There is no life which is not of God,
for God is supreme life and the fount of life.
No life is evil as life but only as it tends to
death. Life knows no death save wickedness
[*nequitia*] which derives its name from nothingness [*ne quidquam*]. For this reason wicked
men are called men of no worth. A life, therefore, which by voluntary defect falls away
from him who made it, whose essence it enjoyed, and, contrary to the law of God, seeks
to enjoy bodily objects which God made to be
inferior to it, tends to nothingness. This is
wickedness, but not because the body as such
is nothing. A corporeal object has some concord between its parts, otherwise it could not
exist at all. Therefore it was made by him who
is the head of all concord. A corporeal object
enjoys a certain degree of peace, due to its
having form. Without that it would be nothing. Therefore he is the creator of matter,
from whom all peace comes, and who is the
uncreated and most perfect form. Matter par-
ticipates in something belonging to the ideal
world, otherwise it would not be matter. To
ask, therefore, who created matter is to ask for
him who is supreme in the ideal world. For
every idea comes from him. Who is he, then,
save the one God, the one truth, the one salvation of all, the first and highest essence from

which all that exists derives existence as such? For all existence as such is good.

22. For that reason death does not come from God. "God did not create death, nor does he take pleasure in the destruction of the living" (Wisdom 1:13). The highest essence imparts existence to all that exists. That is why it is called essence. Death imparts no actual existence to anything which has died. If it is really dead it has indubitably been reduced to nothingness. For things die only in so far as they have a decreasing part in existence. That can be more briefly put in this way: things die according as they become less. Matter is less than any kind of life, since it is life that keeps even the tiniest quantity of matter together in any thing, whether it be the life that governs any particular living thing, or that which governs the entire universe of natural things. Matter is therefore subject to death, and is thereby nearer to nothingness. Life which delights in material joys and neglects God tends to nothingness and is thereby iniquity.

xii, 23. In this way life becomes earthly and carnal. So long as it is so it will not possess the kingdom of God, and what it loves will be snatched from it. It loves what, being matter, is less than life, and, on account of the sinfulness of so doing, the beloved object becomes corruptible, is dissolved and lost to its lover, even as it, in loving a material thing, has abandoned God. It neglected his precepts: Eat this and do not eat that. Therefore it is punished; for by loving inferior things it is given a place among the inferior creatures, being deprived of its pleasures and afflicted with grief. What is bodily grief but the sudden loss of integrity in something which the soul has made a bad use of, so rendering it liable to corruption? And what is spiritual grief but to lose mutable things which the soul enjoyed or hoped to be able to enjoy? This covers the whole range of evil, i.e., sin and its penalty.

24. If the soul, while it continues in the course of human life, overcomes the desires which it has fed to its own undoing by enjoying mortal things, and believes that it has the aid of God's grace enabling it to overcome them, if it serves God with the mind and a good will, it will undoubtedly be restored, and will return from the mutable many to the immutable One. It will be re-formed by the Wisdom which is not formed but has formed all things, and will enjoy God through the spirit, which is the gift of God. It becomes "spiritual man, judging all things and judged of none," "loving the Lord its God with all its heart and all its soul and all its mind, and loving its neighbour not carnally but as itself. He loves himself spiritually who loves God with all that lives within him. On these two commandments hang the whole law and the prophets" (Matt. 22:40).

25. The consequence will be that after the death of the body, which we owe to the primal sin, in its own time and order the body will be restored to its pristine stability; but it will owe its stability not to itself but to the soul whose stability is in God. For the soul too owes its stability not to itself but to God whom it enjoys. Thus it has an ampler life than the body. For the body lives by the soul and the soul by the immutable truth, who is the only Son of God. So even the body lives by the Son of God, because all things live by him. By God's gift, given to the soul, i.e., the Holy Spirit, not only does the soul, which receives it, become sound and peaceful and holy, but the body also will be vivified and will be cleansed completely. The Master himself said: "Cleanse that which is within and that which is without shall be clean" (Matt. 23:26). And the apostle says: "He shall quicken your mortal bodies on account of the Spirit that abideth in you." (Rom. 8:11). Take away sin, and sin's penalty goes too. And where is evil? "O death, where is thy victory? O death, where is thy sting? Being overcomes nothingness, and so death is swallowed up in victory" (I Cor. 15:54-55).

xiii, 26. The evil angel, who is called the devil, will have no power over the sanctified. Even he, so far as he is angel, is not evil, but only so far as he has been perverted by his own will. We must admit that even angels are mutable if God alone is immutable. By willing to

love God rather than themselves angels abide
firm and stable in him and enjoy his majesty,
being gladly subject to him alone. The bad
angel loved himself more than God, refused to
be subject to God, swelled with pride, came
short of supreme being and fell. He became
less than he had been, because, in wishing to
enjoy his own power rather than God's, he
wished to enjoy what was less. He never had
supreme existence for that belongs to God
alone, but he had an ampler existence than he
has now, when he enjoyed that which supremely is. His present existence is not evil
quâ existence, but so far as it is less ample than
it formerly was. To that extent he tends towards extinction. It is no marvel that his loss
occasioned poverty, and poverty envy, which
is the truly diabolical characteristic of the
devil.

xiv, 27. If the defect we call sin overtook a
man against his will, like a fever, the penalty
which follows the sinner and is called condemnation would rightly seem to be unjust. But in
fact sin is so much a voluntary evil that it is not
sin at all unless it is voluntary. This is so obvious that no one denies it, either of the hand-
ful of the learned or of the mass of the un-
learned. We must either say that no sin has
been committed or confess that it has been
willingly committed. No one can rightly deny
that a soul has sinned who admits that it can be
corrected by penitence, that the penitent

should be pardoned, or that he who continues in sin is condemned by the just law of God. Lastly if it is not by the exercise of will that we do wrong, no one at all is to be censured or warned. If you take away censure and warning the Christian law and the whole discipline of religion is necessarily abolished. Therefore, it is by the will that sin is committed. And since there is no doubt that sins are committed, I cannot see that it can be doubted that souls have free choice in willing. God judged that men would serve him better if they served him freely. That could not be so if they served him by necessity and not by free will.

28. The angels accordingly serve God freely. That is to their advantage, not God's. God needs no good thing from others, for all good comes from himself. What is begotten of him is equally divine, begotten not made. Things which are made need his good, i.e., the chief good, the supreme essence. They become less when by sin they are less attracted to him. But they are never entirely separated from him. Otherwise they would not exist at all. Movements of the soul are the affections, depending on the will. Bodily movements are movements in space. Man is said to have been persuaded by the wicked angel, but even so it was his will that consented. If he had consented by necessity, he would have been held guilty of no sin.

xv, 29. The human body was perfect of its

kind before man sinned, but after he had sinned
it became weak and mortal. Though that was
the just punishment for sin, nevertheless it
showed more of the clemency of the Lord
than of his severity. We are thus admonished
that we ought to turn our love from bodily
pleasures to the eternal essence of truth. The
beauty of justice is in complete accord with the
grace of loving-kindness, seeing that we who
were deceived by the sweetness of inferior
goods should be taught by the bitterness of
penalties. For divine providence has so moder-
ated our punishment that even in this corruptible body it is permitted to us to work towards
righteousness, to lay aside all pride and submit
to God alone, not to trust in ourselves but to
commit ourselves to be ruled and defended by
him alone. So with God's guidance a man of
good will can turn the troubles of this present
life to the advantage of courage. Among
abounding pleasures and temporal prosperity,
he may prove and strengthen temperance. In
temptations he may sharpen his prudence, that
he may not only not be led into them, but may
also become more vigilant and more eager in
his love of truth which alone never deceives.

xvi, 30. To heal souls God adopts all kinds
of means suitable to the times which are ordered by his marvellous wisdom. I must not
speak of these, or at least they must be spoken
of only among the pious and the perfect. But
in no way did he show greater loving-kindness

in his dealings with the human race for its good, than when the Wisdom of God, his only Son, coeternal and consubstantial with the Father, deigned to assume human nature; when the Word became flesh and dwelt among us. For thus he showed to carnal people, given over to bodily sense and unable with the mind to behold the truth, how lofty a place among creatures belonged to human nature, in that he appeared to men not merely visibly—for he could have done that in some ethereal body adapted to our weak powers of vision—but as a true man. The assuming of our nature was to be also its liberation. And that no one should perchance suppose that the creator of sex despised sex, he became a man born of a woman.

31. He did nothing by violence, but every thing by persuasion and warning. The old servitude was past and the day of liberty had dawned and man was fitly and helpfully taught how he had been created with free will. By his miracles he, being God, produced faith in God, and by his passion, in the human nature he had assumed, he furthered respect for human nature. Speaking to the multitudes as God he refused to recognize his mother when her coming was announced, and yet, as the Gospel says, he was obedient to his parents (Matt. 12:48, Luke 2:51). In his doctrine the God appeared, and the Man in the various stages of his life. When, as God, he was about

to turn water into wine, he said: "Woman, depart from me; what have I to do with thee? My hour is not yet come" (John 2:4). But when his hour had come when, as man, he should die, he recognized his mother from the Cross and commended her to the disciple whom he loved more than the others (John 19:26-27). The peoples to their own destruction sought riches that minister to pleasures: He determined to be poor. They panted for honours and empires: He refused to be made a king. They thought it a great boon to have sons after the flesh. He scorned marriage and offspring. In their great pride they dreaded insults: He bore with insults of every kind. They thought injuries were not to be endured: what greater injury can there be than that a just and innocent man should be condemned. They execrated bodily pain: He was beaten and tortured. They feared to die: He was condemned to death. They thought a cross the most shameful form of death: He was crucified. All the things which men unrighteously desired to possess, he did without and so made them of no account. All the things which men sought to avoid and so deviated from the search for truth, he endured and so robbed them of their power over us. There is no sin that men can commit which is not either a seeking of what he avoided, or an avoiding of what he bore.

32. His whole life on earth as Man, in the

humanity he deigned to assume, was an education in morals. His resurrection from the dead showed that nothing of human nature can perish, for all is safe with God. It showed also how all things serve the Creator either for the punishment of sin or for the liberation of man, and how the body can serve the soul when the soul is subject to God. When the body perfectly obeys the soul and the soul perfectly serves God, not only is there no evil substance, for that there can never be, but, better still, substance cannot be affected by evil, for it can be so affected only by sin or its punishment. This natural discipline is worthy of the complete faith of less intelligent Christians, and for intelligent Christians it is free from all error.

xvii, 33. This method of teaching fulfils the rule of all rational discipline. For as it teaches partly quite openly and partly by similitudes in word, deed and sacrament, it is adapted to the complete instruction and exercise of the soul. The exposition of mysteries is guided by what is clearly stated. If there was nothing that could not be understood with perfect ease, there would be no studious search for truth and no pleasure in finding it. If there were sacraments in Scripture, and if they were not signs and tokens of truth, action would not be properly related to knowledge. Piety begins with fear and is perfected in love. So in the time of servitude under the old Law the people were constrained by fear and burdened with

many sacraments. That was advantageous for
them in that they might desire the grace of
God which the prophets foretold would come.
When it came, the wisdom of God having assumed human nature and called us into liberty,
few most salutary sacraments were appointed
to maintain the society of the Christian people,
i.e., of the multitude of those set free to serve
the one God. Many things which were im-
posed upon the Hebrew people, i.e., a multitude bound by Law under the same God, are
no longer observed in practice, but they remained valid for faith and are susceptible of
(allegorical) interpretation. They do not now
bind in servile bonds, but they afford the mind
exercise in its freedom.

34. Whoever denies that both Testaments
come from the same God for the reason that
our people are not bound by the same sacraments as those by which the Jews were bound
and still are bound, cannot deny that it would
be perfectly just and possible for one father of
a family to lay one set of commands upon those
for whom he judged a harsher servitude to be
useful, and a different set on those whom he
deigned to adopt into the position of sons. If
the trouble is that the moral precepts under the
old Law are lower and in the Gospel higher,
and that therefore both cannot come from the
same God, whoever thinks in this way may
find difficulty in explaining how a single
physician prescribes one medicine to weaker

patients through his assistants, and another by himself to stronger patients, all to restore health. The art of medicine remains the same and quite unchanged, but it changes its prescriptions for the sick, since the state of their health changes. So divine providence remains entirely without change, but comes to the aid of mutable creatures in various ways, and commands or forbids different things at different times according to the different stages of their disease, whether it be the vice which is the beginning of death, or the final stage when death itself is imminent. In all cases divine providence recalls to its true and essential nature whatever manifests defect, i.e., tends to nothingness, and so strengthens it.

xvii, 35. But you say, Why do they become defective? Because they are mutable. Why are they mutable? Because they have not supreme existence. And why so? Because they are inferior to him who made them. Who made them? He who supremely is. Who is he? God, the immutable Trinity, made them through his supreme wisdom and preserves them by his supreme loving-kindness. Why did he make them? In order that they might exist. Existence as such is good, and supreme existence is the chief good. From what did he make them? Out of nothing. Whatever is must have some form, and though it be but a minimal good it will be good and will be of God. The highest form is the highest good, and the lowest form is the

lowest good. Every good thing is either God
or derived from God. Therefore even the
lowest form is of God. And the same may be
said of species. We rightly praise alike that
which has form and that which has species.
That out of which God created all things had
neither form nor species, and was simply nothing. That which by comparison with perfect
things is said to be without form, but which has
any form at all, however small or inchoate,
is not nothing. It, too, in so far as it has any
being at all, is of God.

36. Therefore, if the world was made out
of some unformed matter, that matter was
made out of absolutely nothing. If it was as
yet unformed, still it was at least capable of
receiving form. By God's goodness it is "form-
able." Even capacity for form is good. The
author of all good things, who gives form, also
gives the capacity for form. All that exists receives existence from God, and that which
does not as yet exist but may do so, receives its
potential existence from God. In other words,
all that is formed receives its form from God,
and from him all that is not yet formed receives power to be formed. Nothing has integrity of nature unless it be whole of its kind.
From God comes all wholeness as every good
thing comes from him.

xix, 37. He whose mental eyes are open
and are not darkened or confused by zeal for
vain verbal victory, understands easily that all

things are good even though they become
vitiated and die; whereas vice and death are
evil. Vice and death do no damage to anything
except by depriving it of soundness, and vice
would not be vice if it did no damage. If vice
is the opposite of wholeness no doubt wholeness is good. All things are good which have
vice opposed to them, and vice vitiates them.
Things which are vitiated are therefore good,
but are vitiated because they are not supremely
good. Because they are good they are of God.
Because they are not supremely good they are
not God. The good which cannot be vitiated
is God. All other good things are of him. They
can of themselves be vitiated because by themselves they are nothing. God keeps them from
being wholly vitiated, or, if vitiated, makes
them whole.

xx,38. The primal vice of the rational soul
is the will to do what the highest and inmost
truth forbids. Thus was man driven from
paradise into the present world, i.e., from eternal things to temporal, from abundance to
poverty, from strength to weakness. Not,
however, from substantial good to substantial
evil, for there is no substanital evil; but from
eternal good to temporal good, from spiritual
to carnal good, from intelligible to sensible
good, from the highest to the lowest good.
There is therefore a good which it is sin for the
rational soul to love because it belongs to a
lower order of being. The sin is evil, not the

substance that is sinfully loved. The tree was not evil which, we read, was planted in the midst of paradise, but the transgression of the divine command was evil, and as a consequence had its just condemnation. But from the tree which was touched contrary to the prohibition came the power to distinguish between good and evil. When the soul has become involved in its sin, it learns, by paying the penalty, the difference between the precept it refused to obey and the sin which it committed. In this way it learns by suffering to know the evil it did not learn to know by avoiding it. By making comparison between its former and its present state it loves more earnestly the good which it loved too little, as is seen from its failure to obey.

39. Vice in the soul arises from its own doing; and the moral difficulty that ensues from vice is the penalty which it suffers. That is the sum-total of evil. To do and to suffer have nothing to do with substance; hence substance is not evil. Water is not evil, nor is a creature that lives in the air. But to throw oneself voluntarily into water and be suffocated, as the drowned man is, is evil. An iron style which has one part for writing with and another part for making deletions is ingeniously manufactured and beautiful in its own way, and most useful to us. But if one wanted to write with the part intended for making deletions, or to make a deletion with the writing end, one would not

cause the style to be evil. One would rightly
blame one's own action. Correct the action and
where will be the evil? Suppose one were sud-
denly to turn one's eyes to look at the mid-day
sun. The eyes would be dazzled and pained;
but neither the sun nor the eyes would for that
reason be evil. They are substances. Careless
looking at the sun and the disturbance that is its
consequence is evil. And there would be no
evil if the eyes had been practised and made fit
to look at the light. Nor is light evil when the
light we see with our eyes is worshipped instead of the light of wisdom which is seen by
the mind. The superstition is evil that serves
the creature rather than the Creator; and there
would be no such evil if the soul recognized its
Creator, subjected itself to him alone, and understood that other things were made subject
to it by him.

40. Every corporeal creature, when possessed by a soul that loves God, is a good thing
of the lowest order, and beautiful in its own
way, for it is held together by form and species. If it is loved by a soul that neglects God,
not even so is it evil in itself. But the sin of so
loving it brings a penalty to him who so loves
it. It involves him in miseries, and feeds him
with fallacious pleasures which neither abide
nor satisfy, but beget torturing sorrows. Time
in all the beauty of its changefulness holds on
its appointed course, and the thing desired escapes him who loved it. It torments him by

passing beyond his power to sense it, and disturbs his mind with errors. For it makes him suppose that the material object which the flesh had wrongly delighted in, and which he had known through the uncertain senses, was the primal form, when in fact it was the lowest form of all; so that, when he thinks, he believes he understands, being deluded by shadowy phantasms. If he does not hold fast to the whole discipline of divine providence but imagines he does, and tries to resist the flesh, he merely reaches the images of visible things. He vainly excogitates vast spaces of light exactly like ordinary light which he sees has fixed limits here, and promises himself a future habitation there. He does not know that he is still entangled in the lust of the eye, and that he is carrying this world with him in his endeavour to go beyond it. He thinks he has reached another world simply by falsely imagining the bright part of this world infinitely extended. One could do the same not only with light but also with water, wine, honey, gold, silver, even with the flesh, blood and bones of animals, and other like things. There is no bodily object seen singly which cannot in thought be infinitely multiplied, and there is nothing which, as we see it, occupies a small space, which cannot by the same faculty of imagination be infinitely extended. It is very easy to execrate the flesh, but very difficult not to be carnally minded.

xxi, 41. By this perversity of the soul, due

to sin and punishment, the whole corporeal creation becomes, as Solomon says: "Vanity of them that are vain, all is vanity. What advantage has man in all his labour which he does under the sun?" (Eccl. 1:2). Not for nothing does he say, "of them that are vain," for if you take away vain persons who pursue that which is last as if it were first, matter will not be vanity but will show its own beauty in its own way, a low type of beauty, of course, but not deceptive. When man fell away from the unity of God the multitude of temporal forms was distributed among his carnal senses, and his sensibilities were multiplied by the changeful variety. So abundance became laborious, and his needs, if one may say so, became abundant, for he pursues one thing after another, and nothing remains permanently with him. So what with his corn and wine and oil, his needs are so multiplied that he cannot find the one thing needful, a single and unchangeable nature, seeking which he would not err, and attaining which he would cease from grief and pain. For then he would have as a consequence the redemption of his body, which no longer would be corrupted. As it is, the corruption of the body burdens the soul, and its earthly habitation forces it to think of many things; for the humble beauty of material objects is hurried along in the order in which one thing succeeds another. The reason why corporeal beauty is the lowest beauty is that its parts cannot all exist simultaneously. Some things give place and others succeed them, and all together complete the number of temporal forms and make of them a single beauty.

xxii, 42. But all this is not evil because it is transient. A line of poetry is beautiful in its own way though no two syllables can be spoken at the same time. The second cannot be spoken till the first is finished. So in due order the end of the line is reached. When the last syllable is spoken the previous ones are not heard at the same time, and yet along with the preceding ones it makes the form and metrical arrangement complete. The art of versifying is not subject to change with time as if its beauty was made up of measured quantities. It possesses, at one and the same time, all the rules for making the verse which consists of successive syllables of which the later ones follow those which had come earlier. In spite of this the verse is beautiful as exhibiting the faint traces of the beauty which the art of poetry keeps steadfastly and unchangeably.

43. Some perverse persons prefer a verse to the art of versifying, because they set more store by their ears than by their intelligence. So many love temporal things and do not look for divine providence which is the maker and governor of time. Loving temporal things they do not want the things they love to pass away. They are just as absurd as anyone would be who, when a famous poem was being recited,

wanted to hear one single syllable all the time.
There are no such hearers of poems, but there
are multitudes of people who think in this way
about historical events. There is no one who
cannot easily hear a whole verse or even a
whole poem; but there is no one who can
grasp the whole order of the ages. Besides, we
are not involved as parts in a poem, but for our
sins we are made to be parts of the secular order. The poem is read for us to judge of it. The
course of history is made up of our labours.
No one who is vanquished in competitive
games finds pleasure in them, but they are honourable because of his dishonour. Here is a sort
of parable of the truth. For no other reason are
we kept from such spectacles than lest we
should be deceived by the shadows of things
and wander from the things themselves where-
of they are shadows. So the condition and
government of the universe displeases only
impious and damned souls, and, in spite of their
misery, it pleases many who are victorious
upon earth, or who look on in heaven without
any risk. Nothing that is just displeases a just
man.

xxiii, 44. Every rational soul is made unhappy by its sins or happy by its well-doing.
Every irrational soul yields to one that is more
powerful, or obeys one that is better, or is on
terms of equality with its equals, exercising
rivals, or harming any it has overcome. Every
body is obedient to its soul so far as permitted

by the merits of the latter or the orderly arrangement of things. There is no evil in the
universe, but in individuals there is evil due to
their own fault. When the soul has been regen-
erated by the grace of God and restored to its
integrity, and made subject to him alone by
whom it was created, its body too will be restored to its original strength, and it will receive power to possess the world, not to be possessed by the world. Then it will have no evil.
For the lowly beauty of temporal changes will
not involve it, for it will have been raised
above change. There will be, as it is written, a
New Heaven and a New Earth, and there souls
will not have to do their part in toiling, but will
reign over the universe. "All things are
yours," says the apostle, "and ye are Christ's
and Christ is God's" (I Cor. 3:21-23). And
again: "The head of the woman is the man, the
head of the man is Christ, and the head of
Christ is God" (I Cor. 11:3). Accordingly,
since the vice of the soul is not its nature but
contrary to its nature, and is nothing else than
sin and sin's penalty, we understand that no nature, or, if you prefer it, no substance or essence, is evil. Nor does the universe suffer any
deformity from the sins and punishments of its
soul. Rational substance which is clear of all
sin and subject to God dominates other things
which are subject to it. But rational substance
which has committed sin is appointed to be
where it is fitting, so that all things should be

glorious, God being the maker and ruler of the universe. The beauty of the created universe is free from all fault because of these three things —the condemnation of sinners, the proving of the just, and the perfecting of the blessed.

xxiv, 45. The treatment of the soul, which God's providence and ineffable loving-kindness administers, is most beautiful in its steps and stages. There are two different methods, authority and reason. Authority demands belief and prepares man for reason. Reason leads to understanding and knowledge. But reason is not entirely absent from authority, for we have got to consider whom we have to believe, and the highest authority belongs to truth when it is clearly known. But because we dwell among temporal things, and love of them is an obstacle to our reaching eternal things, a kind of temporal medicine, calling not those who know but those who believe back to health, has priority by the order, not of nature or its inherent excellence, but of time. Wherever a man falls there he must lie until he is raised up. So we must strive, by means of the carnal forms which detain us, to come to know those of which carnal sense can bring us no knowledge. And by carnal sense I mean eyes, ears, and other bodily senses. To carnal or corporeal forms boys must necessarily and lovingly adhere, adolescents almost necessarily. But with increasing years the necessity disappears.

xxv, 46. Divine providence not only looks
after individuals as it were privately but also
after the whole human race publicly. How it
deals with individuals God knows, who does it,
and they also know, with whom he deals. But
how he deals with the human race God has
willed to be handed down through history and
prophecy. The trustworthiness of temporal
things whether past or future can be believed
rather than known by the intelligence. It is our
duty to consider what men or what books we
are to believe in order that we may rightly
worship God, wherein lies our sole salvation.
Here the first decision must be this: Are we to
believe those who summon us to the worship
of many gods or those who summon us to worship one God? Who can doubt that we ought
rather to follow those who summon us to worship one God, especially since the worshippers
of many gods agree that there is one God who
rules all things? At least the numerical series
begins from the number one. Those, therefore,
are to be followed who say that the one most
high God is the only true God and is to be
worshipped alone. If the truth does not shine
out brightly among them, then, but not till
then, must we go elsewhere. In the realm of
nature there is a presumption of greater authority when all things are brought into unity.
In the human race a multitude has no power
unless by consent, i.e., agreement in unity. So
in religion the authority of those who summon

us to unity ought to be greater and more worthy of being believed.

47. Another thing which must be considered is the dissension that has arisen among men concerning the worship of the one God. We have heard that our predecessors, at a stage in faith on the way from temporal things up to eternal things, followed visible miracles. They could do nothing else. And they did so in such a way that it should not be necessary for those who came after them. When the Catholic Church had been founded and diffused throughout the whole world, on the one hand miracles were not allowed to continue till our time, lest the mind should always seek visible things, and the human race should grow cold by becoming accustomed to things which when they were novelties kindled its faith. On the other hand we must not doubt that those are to be believed who proclaimed miracles, which only a few had actually seen, and yet were able to persuade whole peoples to follow them. At that time the problem was to get people to believe before anyone was fit to reason about divine and invisible things. No human authority is set over the reason of a purified soul, for it is able to arrive at clear truth. But pride does not lead to the perception of truth. If there were no pride there would be no heretics, no schismatics, no circumcised, no worshippers of creatures or of images. If there had not been such classes of

opponents before the people was made perfect
as promised, truth would be sought much less
eagerly.

xxvi, 48. This is the tradition concerning
God's temporal dispensation and his providential care for those who by sin had deservedly
become mortal. First, consider the nature and
education of any individual man who is born.
His first age, infancy, is spent in receiving
bodily nourishment, and it is to be entirely for-
gotten when he grows up. Then follows child-
hood when we begin to have some memories.
To this, adolescence succeeds, when nature al-
lows propagation of offspring and fatherhood.
After adolescence comes young manhood,
which must take part in public duties and be
brought under the laws. Now sins are more
strictly forbidden, and sinners have to undergo
the servile coercion of penalty. In carnal souls
this of itself causes more dreadful onsets of lust,
and wrong-doing is redoubled. For sin has a
double aspect. It is not merely wrong-doing. It
is disobedience. After the labours of young
manhood, a little peace is given to old age.
But it is an inferior age, lacking in lustre, weak
and more subject to disease, and it leads to
death. This is the life of man so far as he lives
in the body and is bound by desires for temporal things. This is called "the old man" and
"the exterior or earthly man," even if he
obtain what the vulgar call felicity in a well-
ordered earthly city, whether ruled by kings

or princes or laws or all of them together. For without these things no people can be well-ordered, not even a people that pursues earthly goods. Even such a people has a measure of beauty of its own.

49. I have described "the old or exterior or earthly man." He may be a moderate man after his kind, or he may transgress the measure of servile justice. Some live thus from the beginning to the end of their days. But some begin in that way, as they necessarily must, but they are reborn inwardly, and with their spiritual strength and increase of wisdom they overcome "the old man" and put him to death, and bring him into subjection to the celestial laws, until after visible death the whole is restored. This is called "the new man," "the inward and heavenly man," whose spiritual ages are marked, not according to years, but according to his spiritual advance. In the first stage he is taught by the rich stores of history which nourish by examples. In the second stage he forgets human affairs and tends towards divine things. He is no longer kept in the bosom of human authority, but step by step by the use of reason he strives to reach the highest unchangeable law. In the third stage he confidently marries carnal appetite to strong reason, and inwardly rejoices in the sweetness of the union. Soul and mind are joined together in chaste union. There is as yet no compulsion to do right, but, even though no one forbids

sin, he has no pleasure in sinning. The fourth stage is similar, only now he acts much more firmly, and springs forth as the perfect man, ready to endure and overcome all the persecutions, tempests and billows of this world. In the fifth stage he has peace and tranquillity on all sides. He lives among the abundant resources of the unchangeable realm of supreme ineffable wisdom. The sixth stage is complete transformation into life eternal, a total forgetfulness of temporal life passing into the perfect form which is made according to the image and likeness of God. The seventh is eternal rest and perpetual beatitude with no distinguishable ages. As the end of "the old man" is death, so the end of "the new man" is eternal life. The "old man" is the man of sin, but the "new man" is the man of righteousness.

xxvii, 50. No one doubts that these two lives are related as follows: A man can live the whole of this life as "the old and earthly man." But no one in this life can live as "the new and heavenly man," but must associate with the "old man." For he must begin there, and must so continue till death, though the old grows weaker and the new progresses. Similarly, the entire human race, whose life, like the life of an individual from Adam to the end of the world, is so arranged by the laws of divine providence that it appears divided among two classes. In one of these is the multitude of the impious who bear the image of the

earthly man from the beginning to the end of
the world. In the other is the succession of the
people devoted to the one God. But from
Adam to John the Baptist they live the life of
the earthly man under a certain form of righteousness. Their history is called the Old Testament having the promise of a kind of earthly
kingdom, which is nothing but the image of
the new people and the New Testament, with
the promise of the kingdom of heaven. Mean-
while the life of this people begins with the
coming of the Lord in humility and goes on till
the day of judgment, when he will come in all
clearness. After the judgment the "old man"
will come to an end, and there will take place
the change that betokens the angelic life. For
we shall all be raised, but we shall not all be
changed (I Cor. 15:51). The pious people will
be raised as they transform the remnants of the
"old man" that cling to them into the "new
man." The impious people who have kept the
"old man" from the beginning to the end, will
be raised in order to be precipitated into the
second death. Those who read diligently can
make out the divisions of the ages. They have
no horror of tares or chaff. For the impious
lives with the pious, and the sinner with the
righteous, so that, by comparing the two, men
may more eagerly rise to seek perfection.

xxviii, 51. If any of the earthly people at
any time had the merit of reaching the illumination of the inward man, he gave to the hu-

man race in his day his aid showing it what that
age required, hinting by prophecy what it was
not opportune to show clearly. Such were the
patriarchs and the prophets. So these discover
who do not behave like children, but who
diligently and piously handle this good and
great secret of the divine-human relations. In
the time of the new people I see that this has
been most carefully provided by great and
spiritual men for the nurselings of the Catholic
Church. They are not to treat publicly of what
they know is not seasonable to be handled before the people. They earnestly feed the multitude of those who are weak and needy with
copious supplies of milky food; and the few
who are wise they feed with stronger meats.
They speak wisdom among the perfect, but
from the carnal and the psychics, though they
be "new men," they keep some things back, because they are still children, but they never lie.
They do not look to vain honours and vain
praise for themselves, but to the advantage of
those with whom they have deserved to be as-
sociated in this life. This is the law of divine
providence that no one is to receive assistance
from his superiors to know and grasp the grace
of God, unless he is prepared with a pure affec-
tion to assist his inferiors to the same. So out of
our sin, which our nature committed in the
first sinful man, the human race is made the
great glory and ornament of the world, and is
so properly governed by the provisions of di-

vine providence that the art of God's ineffable healing turns even the foulness of sin into something that has a beauty of its own.

xxix, 52. We have said enough for the present about the benefit of authority. Let us see how far reason can advance from visible to invisible things in its ascent from temporal to eternal things. We should not vainly behold the beauty of the sky, the order of the stars, the brightness of light, the alternations of day and night, the monthly courses of the moon, the fourfold seasons of the year, the meeting of the four elements, the life-force of seeds begetting forms and numbers, and all things that keep their nature and their appropriate measure each in its own kind. In considering these things there should be no exercise of vain and perishing curiosity, but a step should be taken towards immortal things that abide for ever. The first thing to notice is living nature which senses all these things. Because it gives life to the body it must necessarily excel the body. No mass of matter, however great or however bright, is to be held of much account if it is without life. Any living substance is by the law of nature to be preferred to any inanimate substance.

53. No one doubts that irrational animals also live and feel. So in the human mind the most excellent part is not that which perceives sensible objects but that which judges of sensible objects. Many animals see more sharply

and have a keener sense of corporeal objects than men have. But to judge of bodies belongs not to life that is merely sentient, but to life that has also the power of reasoning. Where the animals are lacking, there is our excellence. It is easy to see that that which judges is superior to that which is judged. For living reason judges not only of sensible things but also of the senses themselves. It knows why the oar dipped in water must appear crooked though it is really straight, and why the eyes must see it in that way. Ocular vision can only tell us that it is so but cannot judge. Wherefore it is manifest that as the life of sense excels the body the life of reason excels both.

xxx, 54. If rational life judges by itself alone, then there is nothing more excellent. But clearly it is mutable, since it can be skilled at one moment and unskilled at another. The more skilled it is the better it judges, and its skill is in proportion to its participation in some art, discipline or wisdom. Now we must ask what is the nature of an art. By an art in this context I would have you understand not something that is observed by experience but something that is found out by reason. There is nothing very remarkable in knowing that sand and lime bind stones more securely together than mud, or that he who would build elegantly, must put a feature that is to be unique in the middle of the building, and, if there are several features, they must be made to correspond, like with like. That is sense-knowledge, but it is not far from reason and truth. We must indeed inquire what is the cause of our being dissatisfied if two windows are placed not one above the other but side by side, and one of them is greater or less than the other, for they ought to have been equal; while, if they are placed one directly above the other, even though they are unlike, the inequality does not offend us in the same way. Why don't we notice very much how much the one is greater or less than the other? If there are three windows, sense itself seems to demand either that they should not be unequal, or that between the largest and the smallest there should be an intermediate one as much larger than the smallest as it is smaller than the largest. In this way we take counsel with nature, as it were, to see what she approves. And here we must observe how that which displeases us only a little when we simply look at it, is rejected when we compare it with what is better. Thus we discover that art in the popular sense is nothing but the memory of things we have experienced and which have given us pleasure, with the addition of some skilled bodily activity. If you lack the skill you can still judge of the works produced even though you cannot produce them. And the power of judging is much better.

55. In all the arts it is symmetry that gives pleasure, preserving unity and making the

whole beautiful. Symmetry demands unity
and equality, the similarity of like parts, or the
graded arrangements of parts which are dis-
similar. But who can find absolute equality or
similarity in bodily objects? Who would venture to say, after due consideration, that any
body is truly and simply one? All are changed
by passing from form to form or from place
to place, and consist of parts each occupying
its own place and extended in space. True
equality and similitude, true and primal unity,
are not perceived by the eye of flesh or by any
bodily sense, but are known by the mind. How
is equality of any kind demanded in bodies,
and how are we convinced that any equality
that may be seen there is far different from
perfect equality, unless the mind sees that
which is perfect? If indeed that which is not
made [*facta*] can be called perfect [*perfecta*].

56. All things which are beautiful to the
senses, whether they are produced by nature
or are worked out by the arts, have a spatial or
temporal beauty, as for example the body and
its movements. But the equality and unity
which are known only by the mind, and according to which the mind judges of corporeal
beauty by the intermediary of the senses, are
not extended in space or unstable in time. It
would be wrong to say that a wheel can be
judged to be round by this standard, while a
little jar cannot, or a jar can but a penny cannot. So in the case of times and motions of cor-

poreal things, it would be ridiculous to say that years can be judged by any standard to be of equal length but months cannot, or that months can and days cannot. Whether a proper movement occupies a larger space of time or is measured by hours or brief minutes, all are judged by one and the same standard of changeless equality. If greater and smaller movements and spatial figures are all judged according to the same standard of equality or similitude or fitness, the standard is greater than all of them in potency. But it is neither greater nor less in a spatial or a temporal sense. If it were greater we should not use the whole of it to judge things that are less. If it were smaller we could not use it to judge things that are larger. As it is, we use the absolute standard of squareness to judge the squareness of a market-place, a stone, a table or a gem. And we use the absolute standard of equality to judge the movements of the feet of a running ant and those of an elephant on the march. Who then can doubt that it is neither greater nor less in a spatial or temporal sense, but in potency surpasses all else? This standard of all the arts is absolutely unchangeable, but the human mind, which is given the power to see the standard, can suffer the mutability of error. Clearly, then, the standard which is called truth is higher than our minds.

xxxi, 57. We must not have any doubt that the unchangeable substance which is above the rational mind, is God. The primal life and primal essence is where the primal wisdom is. This is unchangeable truth which is the law of all the arts and the art of the omnipotent artificer. In perceiving that it cannot judge by itself the form and movement of bodies, the soul ought at the same time to realize that its nature excels the nature of what it judges, but also that it is excelled by the nature according to which it judges and concerning which it cannot judge. I can say why the corresponding members of a single body, one on the one side and the other on the other, ought to be alike, because I delight in absolute equality which I behold not with the bodily eyes but with the mind. And therefore I judge that things seen with the eyes are better the nearer they are in their own kind to the things which I know with my mind. No one can say why these intelligible things should be as they are; and no one in his sober senses should say that they ought to be as they are, as if they could be otherwise.

58. No one, if he rightly understands the matter, will venture to say why intelligible things please us, and why when we are wise we earnestly love them. As we and all rational souls rightly judge of inferior creatures when we judge according to truth, so truth alone judges of us when we cleave to it. Not even the Father judges of truth, for it is not less than he is. What the Father judges he judges

by means of the truth. All things which seek
unity have this rule or form or example, or
whatever it is to be called. For unity alone
bears the whole similitude of him from whom
it has received existence, if it is not incongru-
ous to say "it has received existence" in view
of the significance which attaches to the word
Son. In any case it derives its existence not
from itself but from the first and highest principle which is called the Father: "from whom
the whole family in heaven and on earth is
named" (Eph. 3:15). "The Father therefore
judgeth no man, but hath given all judgment
to the Son" (John 5:22). "The spiritual man
judgeth all things and is himself judged of
none" (I Cor. 2:15), that is by no man, but
only by the law according to which he judges
all things. Wherefore it is most truly said "we
must all appear before the judgment throne of
Christ" (II Cor. 5:10). He judges all things because he is above all when he is with God. He
is with God when he knows most purely and
loves what he knows with all charity. Accordingly, the law is that according to which he
judges all things and concerning which no man
can judge. In the case of temporal laws, men
have instituted them and judge by them, and
when they have been instituted and confirmed
no judge may judge them but must judge according to them. He who draws up temporal
laws, if he is a good and wise man, takes eternal
life into account, and that no soul may judge.

He determines for the time being what is to be commanded and forbidden according to the immutable rules of eternal life. Pure souls may rightly know the eternal law but may not judge it. The difference is that, for knowing, it is enough to see that a thing is *so* and not *so*. For judging, it is necessary in addition to see that a thing can be thus or not thus; as when we say it ought to be thus, or to have been thus, or to be thus in the future, as workmen do with their works.

xxxii, 59. But many stop with what delights men and are unwilling to rise to higher things, so that they may judge why visible things give pleasure. If I ask a workman why, after constructing one arch, he builds another like it over against it, he will reply, I dare say, that in a building like parts must correspond to like. If I go further and ask why he thinks so, he will say that it is fitting, or beautiful, or that it gives pleasure to those who behold it. But he will venture no further. He will bow and direct his eyes downward and not understand the cause for all this. But if I have to do with a man with inward eyes who can see the invisible, I shall not cease to press the query why these things give pleasure, so that he may dare to be the judge of human pleasure. He transcends it and escapes from its control in judging pleasure and not according to pleasure. First I shall ask him whether things are beautiful because they give pleasure, or give pleasure because they are beautiful. Then I shall ask him why they are beautiful, and if he is perplexed, I shall add the question whether it is because its parts correspond and are so joined together as to form one harmonious whole.

60. When he sees that that is so, I shall ask whether they completely achieve the unity they aim at, or fall far short of it, and in a measure misrepresent it. No one who is put on his guard can fail to see that there is no form or material thing which does not have some trace of unity, or that no material thing however beautiful can possibly achieve the unity it aims at, since it must necessarily have its parts separated by intervals of space. If this is so, I shall ask him to tell me where he sees that unity, and what is its source; and if he cannot see it, how does he know what it is that material things imitate but cannot completely achieve. If he says of material things: You would not exist unless some kind of unity held you together, but on the other hand if you were unity itself you would not be material things? the correct reply would be: Whence have you acquired the knowledge of unity according to which you judge material things? Unless you had seen it you would not be able to judge that they come short of it. You would not be right to say that you see it with your bodily eyes, although things do show traces of it, but they come nowhere near it. With the bodily eyes you see nothing but corporeal

things. Therefore it is with the mind that we
see true unity. But where? If it were here
where our body is, it would not be visible to a
man who in eastern parts judges in the same
way about corporeal things. It is not, then, cir-
cumscribed by space. It is present wherever
anyone judges in this way. It is nowhere present spatially, but its potency is nowhere absent.

xxxiii, 61. If corporeal things travesty unity,
we must not trust things that deceive, lest
we fall into the vanities of them that are vain.
Since they deceive by appearing to show to
the eye of flesh the unity which is seen by the
mind alone, we must rather ask whether they
deceive by resembling unity or in failing to
achieve unity. If they achieved it they would
be completely identical with what they imitate. In that case there would be no difference
at all. If that were so there would be no deception. They would be exactly what unity is. In
any case, if you consider the matter closely
they do not actively deceive. He is a deceiver
who wants to appear what he is not. He who,
without willing it, is thought to be other than
he is, is not a deceiver but simply causes mistakes. This is how a deceiver is distinguished
from one who causes mistakes. Every deceiver
has the will to deceive, whether he is believed
or not. But mistakes can be caused by one who
has no intention to deceive. Therefore a corporeal form, which can have no will of its

own, does not deceive. Nor does it cause mistakes if it is not thought to be what it is not.

62. Even the eyes do not cause mistakes, for they can report nothing to the mind except what they actually see. If not only the eyes but also all the bodily senses report simply as they are affected, I know not what more we ought to expect of them. If there are no vain people there will be no vanity. Anyone who thinks that the oar is broken in the water and is restored when it is taken out has nothing wrong with his senses, but he is a bad judge of what they convey to him. By nature he could have seen nothing else in the water, nor ought he to have seen anything else. Air and water differ, so it is proper that sensations should be different according as they relate to things in air and in water. So the eye does its duty correctly, for it was made simply to see. But the mind operates perversely, for it and not the eye was made to contemplate supreme beauty. Such a man as we have been speaking of wants to turn his mind to corporeal things and his eyes to God. He seeks to know carnal things and to see spiritual things. But that is impossible.

xxxiv, 63. That perversity must be corrected. Otherwise things are all out of order, up is down and down is up. Such a man will not be fit for the kingdom of heaven. Do not let us seek the highest in the lowest, nor cleave to the lowest. Let us judge these things lest we

be judged along with them. Let us attribute to
them no more than, as lowest forms, they deserve, lest seeking the first in the last, we be
numbered with the last instead of with the
first. That is no disadvantage to these lowest
things but is a great disadvantage to us. The
divine providential government is not on that
account any less fitting because the unjust are
put in their just place and the foul are fairly
dealt with. If the beauty of visible things
causes us to make mistakes because it consists
in unity but does not completely achieve unity,
let us understand if we can that the mistake
arises not from what they are but from what
they are not. Every corporeal thing is a true
body but a false unity. For it is not supremely
one and does not completely imitate unity.
And yet it would not be a body either if it did
not have some unity. Besides it could have no
unity unless it derived it from supreme unity.

64. Obstinate souls! Give me a single man
who can see without being influenced by imaginations derived from things seen in the
flesh. Give me a single man who can see that
there is no principle of unity but that alone
from which all unity derives, whether it be
complete unity or not. Point me out one who
sees, not one who merely cavils, and wants to
appear to see what he does not see. Give me a
man who can resist the carnal senses and the
impressions which they impose on the mind;

one who can resist human custom and human praise, who suffers the stings of conscience on his bed and restores his soul, who loves not external vanities nor seeks lies; who can say to himself: If there is only one Rome which some Romulus is said to have founded on the Tiber, that is a false Rome which I conjure up in my thoughts. My imaginary Rome is not the real Rome, nor am I really there; otherwise I should know what was taking place there. If there is one sun, that is a false one which I conjure up in thought, for the real sun pursues its course in its appointed place and time. The imaginary sun I place where and when I will. If my friend is one, I conjure up a false image. I do not know where the real one is, but the imaginary one is where I like to put him. I myself am one person, and I feel that my body is here, but in imagination I go where I like, and speak to whom I like. These imaginary things are false, and what is false cannot be known. When I contemplate them and believe in them, I do not have knowledge, because what I contemplate with the intelligence must be true, and not by any possibility what are commonly called phantasms. Whence, then, is my mind full of illusions? Where is the truth which the mind beholds? It can be replied to one who thinks in this way that that is the true light which enables you to know that these things are not true. By the true light you see the

unity whereby you judge whatever you see to
be one. But it is quite a different thing from
any mutable thing you can see.

xxxv, 65. If your mind eagerly pants to behold these things, keep quiet. Do not strive except against being accustomed to material
things. Conquer that habit and you are victorious over all. We seek unity, the simplest thing
of all. Therefore let us seek it in simplicity
of heart. "Be still and know that I am God"
(Ps. 46:10). This is not the stillness of idleness
but of thought, free from space and time.
Swelling fleeting phantasms do not permit us
to see abiding unity. Space offers us something
to love, but time steals away what we love and
leaves in the soul crowds of phantasms which
incite desire for this or that. Thus the mind becomes restless and unhappy, vainly trying to
hold that by which it is held captive. It is sum-
moned to stillness so that it may not love the
things which cannot be loved without toil. So
it will master them. It will hold them and not
be held by them. "My yoke," says the Lord,
"is light" (Matt. 11:30). He who is subject to
that yoke has everything else subject to himself. He will not labour, for what is subject
does not resist. Men could be masters of this
world if they were willing to be the sons of
God, for God has given them the power to
become his sons. But the unhappy friends of
this world so fear to be separated from its em-

brace that nothing is more toilsome to them than to be at rest.

xxxvi, 66. Whoever clearly sees that falsehood is thinking something is what it is not, knows that truth is that which declares what is. If material things deceive us in so far as they fall short of the unity which they demonstrably imitate, we naturally approve them; for that is the principle from which all unity derives, and to resemble which all things strive. We equally disapprove all that departs from unity and tends towards its opposite. We can understand that there is something so resembling the sole unity and principle of all unity that it coincides with it and is identical with it. This is truth, the Word that was in the beginning [*in principio*], the divine Word that was with God. If falsehood springs from things which imitate unity, not in so far as they imitate it but in so far as they cannot achieve it, the truth which does achieve it, and is identical with it, is unity and manifests unity as it is in reality. Hence, it is rightly called unity's Word and Light. Other things may be said to be like unity in so far as they have being, and so far they are also true. But this is itself the complete likeness of unity, and is therefore truth. Truth makes all things true which are true, and likeness makes things like which are alike. Truth is the form of all things which are true, and likeness of all things which are alike,

since things are true in so far as they have being, and have being in so far as they resemble
the source of all unity, that is, the form of all
things that have being, which is the supreme
likeness of the principle. It is also perfect truth
because it is without any unlikeness.

67. Falsehood arises not because things deceive us, for they can show the beholder nothing but their form, and that they have received
according to their position in the scale of
beauty. Nor do the senses deceive us, for when
they are in contact with natural objects they
report to their presiding mind nothing but the
impressions formed upon them. It is sin which
deceives souls, when they seek something that
is true but abandon or neglect truth. They
love the works of the artificer more than the
artificer or his art, and are punished by falling
into the error of expecting to find the artificer
and his art in his works, and when they cannot
do so they think that the works are both the
art and the artificer. God is not offered to
the corporeal senses, and transcends even the
mind.

xxxvii, 68. This is the origin of all impiety
of sinners who have been condemned for their
sins. Not only do they wish to scrutinize the
creation contrary to the commandment of
God, and to enjoy it rather than God's law and
truth—that was the sin of the first man who
misused his free will—but in their state of condemnation they also make this addition to their

sin. They not only love but also serve the
creature rather than the Creator, and worship
the parts of the creation from the loftiest to
the lowliest. Some worship the soul in place of
the most high God, the first intellectual creature which the Father made by means of the
truth, that it might ever behold the truth, and
beholding the truth might also behold himself
whom the truth resembles in every way.
Next, men come to the living creature through
which God eternal and unchangeable makes
things visible and temporal in the realm of becoming. Then they slip further down and worship animals and even material things, among
which they first choose the more beautiful,
above all the heavenly bodies. Some are satisfied with the sun, the most obvious of the
heavenly bodies. Others think the moon
worthy of religious veneration because of its
brightness. It is nearer to us, we are told, and
so is felt to have a form that is closer to us.
Others add the rest of the stars and the sky as
a whole with its constellations. Others join the
air to the ethereal sky and make their souls
subordinate to these two superior corporeal
elements. But those think themselves most religious who worship the whole created universe, that is, the world with all that is in it,
and the life which inspires and animates it,
which some believe to be corporeal, others incorporeal. The whole of this together they
think to be one great God, of whom all things

are parts. They have not known the author
and maker of the universe. So they abandon
themselves to idols, and, forsaking the works
of God, they are immersed in the works of
their own hands, all of them visible things.

xxxviii, 69. There is another worse and
lower idolatry which worships phantasms.
Whatever the erring soul in its swelling pride
can imagine, they hold as an object of religious
worship until at last some conclude that nothing at all should be worshipped, and that men
err who allow themselves to get involved in
superstition and miserable servitude. But these
opinions are vain. They cannot make themselves free. There remain the vices, and they
are drawn towards the notion of worshipping
them. They are slaves of desire in three forms
—desire of pleasure, desire of excelling, desire
of novel entertainment. I say that there is no
man who holds that there is nothing he ought
to worship, who is not the slave of carnal
pleasures, or seeks vain power, or is madly delighted by some showy spectacle. So, without
knowing it, they love temporal things and
hope for blessedness therefrom. Whether he
will or no, a man is necessarily a slave to the
things by means of which he seeks to be happy.
He follows them whithersoever they lead, and
fears anyone who seems to have the power to
rob him of them. Now a spark of fire or a tiny
animal can do that. In short, not to mention innumerable adverse possibilities, time itself must

snatch away all transient things. Now since the world includes all temporal things, those who think to escape servitude by not worshipping anything are in fact the slaves of all kinds of worldly things. In their present extremity unhappy men are so placed that they allow their vices to lord it over them, and are condemned for their lust, pride or curiosity, or for two of them or all together. Nevertheless, so long as they are in this stadium of human life they may attack these vices and overcome them, if they begin by believing what they cannot yet grasp with the understanding, and thereby cease to love the world. As it is written: "All that is in the world is lust of the flesh, lust of the eyes, and ambition of this world" (I John 2:16). Three classes of men are thus distinguished; for lust of the flesh means those who love the lower pleasures, lust of the eyes means the curious, and ambition of this world denotes the proud.

71. The threefold temptation of the Man whom the truth assumed has given us an example for our warning. "Bid these stones that they become bread," says the tempter. To which our one and only teacher replies: "Man does not live by bread alone, but by every word of God" (Matt. 4:3-4). So he taught that desire for pleasure should be brought under, and that we should not yield even to hunger. But possibly some one who could not be overcome by the pleasures of the flesh could

be by the pomp of temporal domination. So all the kingdoms of the world were shown, and the tempter said: "All these things will I give thee, if thou wilt fall down and worship me." To this it was replied: "Thou shalt worship the Lord thy God and him only shalt thou serve" (Matt. 4:9-10). So was pride trodden under foot. Moreover the utmost enticements of curiosity were also overcome. For the only reason for urging him to cast himself down from the pinnacle of the temple was that he might have a remarkable experience. Not even so was he overcome, but in order that we should understand that to know God there is no need to explore divine power by subjecting it to visible experiments, he replied: "Thou shalt not tempt the Lord thy God" (Matt. 4:7). Wherefore he who is inwardly fed upon the Word of God does not seek pleasure in the desert. He who is subject to the one God does not seek glory on the mountain, that is, in earthly elation. He who begins to cleave to the eternal spectacle of unchangeable truth is not thrown down by the pinnacle of the body, that is, the eyes, to seek to know inferior and temporal things.

xxix, 72. What obstacle then remains to hinder the soul from recalling the primal beauty which it abandoned, when it can make an end of its vices? The Wisdom of God extends from end to end with might. By wisdom the great Artificer knit his works together

with one glorious end in view. His goodness
has no grudging envy against any beauty from
the highest to the lowest, for none can have
being except from him alone. So that no one
is utterly cast away from the truth who has in
him the slightest vestige of truth. What is it
about bodily pleasure that holds us fast? You
will find that it is agreeableness. Disagreeable
things beget grief and agreeable things beget
pleasure. Seek therefore the highest agreeableness. Do not go abroad. Return within yourself. In the inward man dwells truth. If you
find that you are by nature mutable, transcend
yourself. But remember in doing so that you
must also transcend yourself even as a reasoning soul. Make for the place where the light of
reason is kindled. What does every good reasoner attain but truth? And yet truth is not
reached by reasoning, but is itself the goal of
all who reason. There is an agreeableness than
which there can be no greater. Agree, then,
with it. Confess that you are not as it is. It has
to do no seeking, but you reach it by seeking,
not in space, but by a disposition of mind, so
that the inward man may agree with the in-
dwelling truth in a pleasure that is not low
and carnal but supremely spiritual.

73. If you do not grasp what I say and
doubt whether it is true, at least make up your
mind whether you have any doubt about your
doubts. If it is certain that you do indeed have
doubts, inquire whence comes that certainty.

It will never occur to you to imagine that it comes from the light of the sun, but rather from that "true light which lighteth every man that cometh into the world." It cannot be seen with these eyes, nor with the eyes which seem to see the phantasms of the brain, but with those that can say to phantasms: You are not the thing I am seeking. Nor are you the standard by which I put you in your rightful place, disapproving of all that is base in you, and approving of all that is beautiful. The standard according to which I approve and disapprove is still more beautiful, so I approve more highly of it and prefer it not only to you but to all those bodily shapes from which you spring. Now think of the rule in this way. Everyone who knows that he has doubts knows with certainty something that is true, namely, that he doubts. He is certain, therefore, about *a* truth. Therefore everyone who doubts whether there be such a thing as *the* truth has at least *a* truth to set a limit to his doubt; and nothing can be true except truth be in it. Accordingly, no one ought to have doubts about the existence of *the* truth, even if doubts arise for him from every possible quarter. Wherever this is seen, there is light that transcends space and time and all phantasms that spring from spatial and temporal things. Could this be in the least destroyed even if every reasoner should perish or grow old among inferior carnal things? Reasoning does not create truth but discovers it. Before it is discovered it abides in itself; and when it is discovered it renews us.

xl, 74. So the inward man is reborn, and the outward man decays day by day. The inward man regards the outward man and sees that he is base by comparison. Nevertheless, in his own kind he is beautiful and rejoices in what is convenient for the body, destroying what he converts to his own good, e.g., the nourishment he takes for the sake of his body. That which is destroyed, i.e., loses its form, passes into the workshop of his members, nourishes what needs nourishment and is transformed as is suitable. Somehow the processes of life make a selection. Some things which are suitable are assumed into the structure of the visible body and make it beautiful. Those which are not suitable are cast out by appropriate means. The most filthy part is returned to the earth to assume other forms. Something is exhaled by the whole body. Another part receives the latent numerical qualities of the living person, and is fitted to result in offspring. Prompted by the agreement of two bodies or by some like phantasm, it flows from the genital organs in basest pleasure, though not without the co-operation of the head. Within the mother over a fixed period of time it takes shape, and the members assume their proper place and function, and if they preserve their proper measure and symmetry and colour is

added, a body is born which is called comely
and is keenly loved by those who take delight
in it. But what gives pleasure is not so much
the mobile form as the life which causes the
mobility. For if the child loves us it strongly
attracts us. If it hates us we are angry and cannot endure it, even though its form be such as
we might enjoy. All this is the realm of pleasure and of beauty of the lowest grade. It is
subject to corruption, otherwise it would be
mistaken for the supreme beauty.

75. Divine providence is at hand to show
that the beauty of the human form is not evil,
because it exhibits manifest traces of the primal
numbers, though divine wisdom is not numbered among them; but also that it is beauty
of the lowest grade, for mixed up with it are
griefs and diseases, distortions of limbs, darkness of colour, and conflicts and dissensions of
mind. By these things we are admonished that
we must seek something unchangeable. These
evils providence brings about by the agency of
inferior beings who find their pleasure in doing this, and whom the divine Scriptures call
avengers and ministers of wrath, though they
themselves do not know the good that is being
done by means of them. Like these are men
who rejoice in the miseries of others, and make
sport and mocking spectacles by subverting
others or by leading them astray. In all these
things the good are admonished and exercised,
and they are victorious, triumphant and regal.

But the bad are deceived and tortured. They are vanquished, condemned and made to be slaves, not of the one most high Lord of all, but of his lowest servants, the bad angels who feed upon the griefs and misery of the damned, and in return for their malevolence are tortured when they see the good set free.

76. All have their offices and limits laid down so as to ensure the beauty of the universe. That which we abhor in any part of it gives us the greatest pleasure when we consider the universe as a whole. When we are judging a building we ought not to consider one angle only. So when we are judging a good-looking man we should not take account only of his hair. And with one who is making a good speech we should not merely pay attention to the motion of his hands. When we are thinking of the moon's course we should not study its phases over a period of merely three days. The very reason why some things are inferior is that though the parts may be imperfect the whole is perfect, whether its beauty is seen stationary or in movement. It must all be considered if we wish to reach a right judgment. If our judgment concerning the whole or the part is true, it is also beautiful. It is superior to the whole world, and in so far as our judgment is true we cling to no part of the world. When we are wrong, and pay exclusive attention to the part, our judgment is in itself base. The colour black in a picture may very

well be beautiful if you take the picture as a whole. So the entire contest of human life is fittingly conducted by the unchanging providence of God who allots different rôles to the vanquished and the victorious, the contestants, the spectators, and the tranquil who contemplate God alone. In all these cases there is no evil except sin and sin's penalty, that is, a voluntary abandonment of highest being, and toil among inferior beings which is not voluntary; in other words, freedom from justice and slavery under sin.

xli, 77. The outward man is destroyed either by the progress of the inward man, or by his own failure. When he is destroyed by the progress of the inward man, the whole man is reformed and made better, and is restored to his integrity "at the last trump." No longer will he corrupt or be corrupted. By his own failure he is cast down among corruptible beauties which rank as penalties. Do not be surprised if I still call them beautiful things, for everything is beautiful that is in due order. As the apostle says: "All order is of God" (Rom. 13:2). We must admit that a weeping man is better than a happy worm. And yet I could speak at great length without any falsehood in praise of the worm. I could point out the brightness of its colouring, the slender rounded shape of its body, the fitness of its parts from front to rear, and their effort to preserve unity as far as is possible in so lowly a creature. There is nothing anywhere about it that does not correspond to something else that matches it. What am I to say about its soul animating its tiny body? Even a worm's soul causes it to move with precision, to seek things suitable for it, to avoid or overcome difficulties as far as possible. Having regard always to the sense of safety, its soul hints much more clearly than its body at the unity which creates all natures. I am speaking of any kind of living worm. Many have spoken fully and truly in praise of ashes and dung. What wonder is it then if I say that a man's soul, which, wherever it is and whatever its quality, is better than any body, is beautifully ordered, and that other beauties arise even from the penalties it undergoes? For when it is unhappy it is not where it is fitting that only the happy should be, but where it is fitting that the unhappy should be.

78. Henceforth, let no one deceive us. Whatever is rightly to be blamed is spurned in comparison with what is better. Every existing thing however lowly is justly praised when it is compared with nothingness. Nothing is good if it can be better. If we can be in good case having the truth itself, our state is bad if we have only a trace of truth, and much worse if the trace is extremely slight as when we adhere to fleshly pleasures. Let us conquer the blandishments and troubles of desire. If we are men let us subdue this woman, *Cupiditas*. With our guidance she will herself become better

and be called no longer Cupidity but Temperance. When she leads and we follow she is called Lust and we Rashness and Folly. Let us follow Christ our Head, that she whose head we are may follow us. This precept can be laid upon women too, not by marital but by fraternal right. In Christ there is neither male nor female. Women too have some virile quality whereby they can subdue feminine pleasures, and serve Christ and govern desire. This is exemplified by many godly widows and virgins, and in many too who are married but who by the dispensation of the Christian people preserve conjugal rights in the bond of fraternity. God bids us dominate desire, and exhorts us and gives us the power to be restored to our own possession. If therefore by negligence or impiety a man, i.e., mind and reason, is subdued by desire he will be a base and unhappy man. His destiny in this life and his ordained place hereafter will be where the most high Ruler and Lord will apportion him. The universal creation may not be stained by any filthiness.

xlii, 79. Let us therefore walk while we have the day, i.e., while we can use reason. Let us turn to God so that we may deserve to be illumined by his Word, the true light, and that darkness may not take possession of us. Day is the presence of the "light that lighteth every man coming into the world" (John 1:9). "Every man," says Scripture, meaning everyone who can use reason, and who, when he has fallen, can earnestly seek to rise. If fleshly pleasure is loved, let it be carefully considered and vestigial traces of number will be recognized in it. We must, then, seek the realm where number exists in complete tranquillity; for there existence is, above all, unity. And if number is found in living movement, as for example in growing seeds, it will be even more wonderful than when found in corporeal things. If in seeds number could change and swell as seeds themselves do, half a tree would grow from half a fig-seed. Whole and complete animals would not be produced except from complete animal seeds (as they are in the case of the litters of certain animals); and a single tiny seed would not have the power to multiply its own kind innumerably. Obviously, from a single seed, according to the nature of each, crops can propagate crops, woods woods, herds herds, and peoples peoples throughout the ages, so that there is not a single leaf or hair in all that rhythmic succession, the reason for which did not exist in the first single seed. Again, think of the rhythmic and pleasantly beautiful sounds transmitted by the air when the nightingale sings. And yet the soul of that bird could not produce them so freely when it pleased, unless it had them incorporeally impressed upon it by the life force. This can be observed in other living creatures which lack reason but do not lack sense. There is none of them which does not in the sound of its voice or in some other movement or activity of its members show something rhythmical and in its own fashion orderly, not indeed by reason of any knowledge, but by reason of the deep ties of nature which are arranged by the unchangeable law of numbers.

xliii, 80. Let us return to ourselves and pass over the things we have in common with trees and beasts. The swallow builds its nest in one way, and every kind of bird has its own way of building its nest. What is it in us that enables us to judge all these, the plan they are following and how far they accomplish it; to judge ourselves, too, in our buildings and other activities of the body, as if we were lords of all such things? What gives us these innumerable thoughts? What is it within us that knows that these corporeal things are relatively great or small, that every body can be halved, whatever size it may have, and even then may be subdivided into innumerable parts? If a grain of millet bears the same relation to one of its parts as our body bears to the world, it is as great in respect of that part as the world is in respect of us. And the world is full of designs and is beautiful not because of its size but because of the reason that is in it. It seems great not because of its quantity but by comparison with our smallness and the smallness of the living things it contains. These again can be infinitely divided, and are small not in themselves but by comparison with other things and above all with the universe itself. Nor is it different with respect to lengths of time. As in the case of space, every length of time can be halved. However brief it may be it has a beginning, a duration and an end. So it must have a middle point, being divided at the point where it draws nearer to the end. The short syllable is short by comparison with a long syllable, and the hour is short in winter when compared with a summer hour. So the space of a single hour is short by comparison with a day. So a day is short by comparison with a month, a month with a year, a year with a lustrum, a lustrum with the larger circles of time and they with universal time. The whole rhythmic succession and gradation in space and time is judged to be beautiful not by its size or length but by its ordered fitness.

81. The mode of order lives in perpetual truth. It has no bulk or temporal process. By its potency it is greater than all space, and by its eternity it remains changeless above the flux of time. And yet without it, vast bulk can have no unity, and length of time cannot be kept in the straight path. There could be neither matter nor motion. It is the principle of unity, having neither size nor change whether finite or infinite. It has not one quality here and another there, or one now and another afterwards; for it is supremely the unique Father of

Truth and Father of Wisdom, which is like the
Father in all respects. Hence it is called his
similitude and image because it comes from
him. It is rightly called also the Son, and from
him other things proceed. But before him is the
universal form perfectly identical with the
unity from which it springs, so that all other
things, so far as they have being and resemble
unity, are made according to that form.

xliv, 82. Some things are made comform-
able to that first form such as rational and
intellectual creatures, among whom man is
rightly said to be made in the image and likeness of God. Not otherwise could he behold
unchangeable truth with his mind. But other
things are made through the first form but are
not in its image. If the rational creature serve
its creator by whom, through whom, and to
whom it was made, all other things will serve
it. Life, which is next in the scale below soul,
will lend aid in commanding the body. And
the soul will even rule over the body, that last
and lowest being, for the body will yield to its
will in all things and will give no trouble; because the soul will not seek its happiness from
the body or by it, but will receive happiness
by itself from God. So the body too will be
reformed and sanctified, and the soul will rule
it without loss or corruption and without
any burden of difficulty. "In the resurrection
they neither marry nor are given in marriage
but will be like the angels in heaven"

(Matt. 22:30). "Meats for the belly and the belly for meats, but God will destroy both it and them" (I Cor. 6:13). "The kingdom of God is not eating and drinking, but righteousness and peace and joy" (Rom. 14:17).

xlv, 83. Wherefore even in bodily pleasure we find something to teach us to despise it, not because the body is evil by nature, but because it is shameful for a being who can cleave to higher things and enjoy them to be the sport of love of the lowest good. When a charioteer loses control and pays the penalty for his rashness he accuses his equipment. But let him implore aid; let him take command of the situation; let him control his steeds which are making a spectacle of his downfall and bid fair to bring about his death if no help supervenes. Let him get back into his place in the chariot, and take control of the reins, and tame his horses and rule them more cautiously. Then he will realize how well the chariot had been made with all its equipment, which by his ruinous handling brought danger upon himself and left the course of becoming moderation. So in paradise the greediness of the soul which badly used its body produced weakness. For it snatched at forbidden food against the prescription of the physician, in following which salvation is to be found.

84. If in the very weakness of visible flesh, where no happy life can be, some pointer towards happiness can be found, because the

form of it reaches from the top to the bottom
of the scale of existence, much more can a
pointer be found in the search for rank and excellence, even in the pride and vain pomp of
this world. For what else does a man seek in
this case but to be if possible the sole lord of all
things, perversely imitating Almighty God?
If he submissively imitated him by living according to his commandments, God would
put all other things under him, and he would
not reach such deformity as to fear a little animal even while he wants to rule over men.
Pride in a manner seeks unity and omnipotence, but in the realm of temporal things,
where all things are transient like a shadow.

85. We want to be unconquered and rightly
so, for the nature of our mind is unconquerable though only as we are subject to God in
whose image we are made. But his commandments had to be observed, and if they were
obeyed no one would overcome us. But now
while the woman to whose words we basely
consented is subject to the pains of childbirth,
we labour on the ground and are disgracefully
overcome by anything that can trouble or disturb us. We do not want to be overcome by
men, but we cannot overcome anger. What
more execrable baseness can there be? We admit that we are men, and even a vicious man is
better than vice. How much more honourable
it would be to be conquered by a man than by
a vice? Who would doubt that envy is a mon-

strous vice which must necessarily torture and subdue anyone who is unwilling to be conquered in temporal things? It is better that a man should overcome us than that we should be overcome by envy or any other vice.

xlvi, 86. He who has overcome his vices cannot be overcome by man either. Only he is overcome who has what he loves snatched from him by his adversary. He who loves only what cannot be snatched from him is indubitably unconquerable, and is tortured by no envy. He loves what many have come to know and to love, thereby deserving to be congratulated. For he loves God with all his heart and with all his soul and with all his mind, and his neighbour as himself. God does not grudge his becoming as he is himself. Rather he even helps him as much as possible. He cannot lose his neighbour whom he loves as himself, for he does not love even in himself the things that appear to the eyes or to any other bodily sense. So he has inward fellowship with him whom he loves as himself.

87. The rule of love is that one should wish his friend to have all the good things he wants to have himself, and should not wish the evils to befall his friend which he wishes to avoid himself. He shows this benevolence towards all men. No evil must be done to any. Love of one's neighbour worketh no evil (Rom. 13:10). Let us then love even our enemies as we are commanded, if we wish to be truly un-

conquered. For no man is unconquerable in himself, but by the unchangeable law which makes free those who serve it and them only. What they love cannot be taken from them, and by that fact alone they are rendered unconquerable and perfect men. If a man were to love another not as himself but as a beast of burden, or as the baths, or as a gaudy or garrulous bird, that is for some temporal pleasure or advantage he hoped to derive, he must serve not a man but, what is much worse, a foul and detestable vice, in that he does not love the man as a man ought to be loved. When that vice is dominant it leads to the lowest form of life or rather to death.

88. Man is not to be loved by man even as brothers after the flesh are loved, or sons, or wives, or kinsfolk, or relatives, or fellow citizens. For such love is temporal. We should have no such connections as are contingent upon birth and death, if our nature had remained in obedience to the commandments of God and in the likeness of his image. It would not have been relegated to its present corrupt state. Accordingly, the Truth himself calls us back to our original and perfect state, bids us resist carnal custom, and teaches that no one is fit for the kingdom of God unless he hates these carnal relationships. Let no one think that is inhuman. It is more inhuman to love a man because he is your son and not because he is a man, that is, not to love that in him

which belongs to God, but to love that which belongs to yourself. What marvel if he who loves his private advantage and not the commonweal does not obtain a kingdom? Someone will say he should love both, but God says he must love one. Most truly says the Truth: "No man can serve two masters" (Matt. 6:24). No one can perfectly love that *to* which we are called unless he hate that *from* which we are called. We are called to perfect human nature as God made it before we sinned. We are recalled from love of what we have deserved by sinning. Therefore we must hate that from which we choose to be set free.

89. If we are ablaze with love for eternity we shall hate temporal relationships. Let a man love his neighbour as himself. No one is his own father or son or kinsman or anything of the kind, but is simply a man. Whoever loves another as himself ought to love that in him which is his real self. Our real selves are not bodies. So we are not to desire and set great store by a man's body. Here, too, the precept is valid: Thou shalt not covet thy neighbour's property. Whoever, then, loves in his neighbour anything but his real self does not love him as himself. Human nature is to be loved whether it be perfect or in process of becoming perfect, but without any condition of carnal relationship. All are related who have one God for their Father and who love him and do his will. And all are fathers and sons to one

another, fathers when they take thought for
others, sons when they obey, but above all
they are brothers because one Father by his
Testament calls them to one inheritance.

xlvii, 90. Why should not he be unconquered who in loving man loves nothing but
the man, the creature of God, made according
to his image? And how can he fail to discover
the perfect nature he loves, since God is perfect? For example, if anyone loves a good
singer, not this or that particular one but any
good singer, being himself a perfect singer, he
wants all to be such, while at the same time
preserving his own power to do what he loves,
for he too sings well. But if he is envious of
any good singer, he does not love good singing
for itself but for the praise or some other advantage he wishes to obtain by singing well.
But that advantage can be diminished or indeed taken away if another sings well. He who
is envious of a good singer does not love him
for his singing; and on the other hand, he who
lacks talent does not sing well. This could be
much more fitly said of one who lives rightly,
because he can envy no one. For the reward
of right living is the same for all, and it is not
made less when many obtain it. A time may
come when a good singer cannot sing properly, and requires another's voice to show
what he loves. He might be at a banquet
where it was wrong for him to sing, but where
he might properly hear another sing. But it is

never improper to live aright. Whoever does
this and loves it, not only does not envy those
who imitate him, but also treats them with the
greatest possible kindness and good will. But
he does not stand in any need of them. What he
loves in them he himself completely and perfectly possesses. So when a man loves his
neighbour as himself, he is not envious of him
any more than he is envious of himself. He
gives him such help as he can as if he were
helping himself. But he does not need him any
more than he needs himself. He needs God
alone, by cleaving to whom he is happy. No
one can take God from him. He, then, is most
truly and certainly an unconquered man who
cleaves to God, not indeed that he may merit
any extra good thing from him, but because
for him to cleave to God is itself good.

91. Such a man, so long as he is in this life,
uses his friend to repay favours received, his
enemy to cultivate patience, anyone at all in
order to exercise beneficence, and all men as
objects of benevolence. Though he does not
love temporal things, he uses them rightly
himself, and takes thought for men according
to the lot of each, if he cannot treat them all
alike. So if he is more ready to speak to one of
his friends than to anyone else, it is not because he loves him more, but because he has
greater confidence in addressing him, and op-
portunity opens the door. He treats those who
are devoted to temporal concerns all the better

because he is himself less bound to temporal
things. If he cannot help all whom he loves
equally without preferring to benefit those
who are more closely related to him, he is unjust. Relationship of mind is a greater thing
than relationships due to the place or time
where or when we were born in the flesh. But
the relationship which binds all together is the
most important of all. He is not made sorrow-
ful by the death of anyone, for he who loves
God with all his mind knows that nothing can
perish for him unless it perish also in the sight
of God. But God is Lord of the living and the
dead. He is not made unhappy by the unhappi-
ness of another, any more than he is made just
by the justice of another. As no one can take
from him God and justice, so no one can take
from him his happiness. If at any time he is
touched with feeling for another's danger or
error or grief, he lets it go so far as to help or
correct or console that other, but not to sub-
vert himself.

92.   In all laborious duties he cherishes the
certain expectation of rest to come, and so is
not crushed. What can harm him who can
make a good use even of an enemy? He does
not fear enmities because he is guarded and
protected by God who has given both the
command and the ability to love enemies. In
tribulations he feels it is a small thing not to be
saddened. Rather he even rejoices, knowing
that "tribulation worketh patience, and pa-

tience experience, and experience hope, and hope maketh not ashamed, because the love of God is shed abroad in our hearts by the Holy Spirit, which is given unto us" (Rom. 5:3-5). Who can hurt such a man? Who can subdue him? In prosperity he makes moral progress, and in adversity learns to know the progress he has made. When he has abundance of mutable goods he does not put his trust in them; and when they are withdrawn he gets to know whether or not they had taken him captive. Usually when we have them we imagine that we do not love them, but when they begin to leave us we discover what manner of men we are. We have a thing without loving it when we can let it go without grieving. He who by excelling obtains what he will grieve to lose, seems to be victorious but is in reality vanquished; and he who by giving way obtains what he cannot unwillingly lose is really victorious though he seem to be vanquished.

xlviii, 93. He who delights in liberty seeks to be free from the love of mutable things. He who delights to rule should submissively cleave to God, the sole ruler of all things, loving God more than himself. This is perfect justice, to love the better things more and the lesser things less. He should love a wise and perfect soul because it has the quality of justice, and a foolish soul because it has the power to become wise and perfect. He ought not to love even himself if he is foolish; for he

who loves himself when he is foolish will make
no progress towards wisdom. No one will become what he desires to be unless he hates himself as he is. But until he reaches wisdom and
perfection he bears with the folly of his neighbour as he would bear with his own, suppos-
ing he were foolish and at the same time a
lover of wisdom. Wherefore, if even pride itself is the shadow of true liberty and true
royalty, by it also divine providence reminds
us what we are worth when we are stained
with vice, and to what we must return when
we have been corrected.

xlix, 94. All curiosity with regard to spectacles aims at nothing else than the joy of
knowing things. What, then, is more wonderful and beautiful than truth? Every spectator
admits that he wants to reach truth. Hence he
takes great care not to be deceived, and vaunts
himself if he shows more acuteness and vivacity
than others in watching and learning and judging. Men carefully and closely watch a juggler
who professes nothing but deceit. If his tricks
elude discovery they are delighted with the
cleverness of the man who hoodwinks them. If
he did not know how to mislead those who
were looking on, or was believed not to know,
no one would applaud. But any of the people
who catches him out thinks himself worthy of
greater praise than the juggler for no other reason than that he could not be deceived or taken
in. If many see through the trick the juggler is

not praised, but the rest who cannot see it are laughed at. So the palm is always awarded to knowledge, to the comprehension of truth. But no one can reach truth who looks for it outside the mind.

95. When we are asked which is better, truth or falsehood, we answer with one voice that truth is better. And yet we are so sunk in trifles and baseness that we are much more ready to cling to jests and games in which deception, not truth, delights us, than to the precepts of the truth itself. So by our own judgment and out of our own mouth we are sentenced because we approve one thing by reason and pursue another in our vanity. So long as a thing is a matter of fun and games, we know that it arouses laughter when it counterfeits truth. But when we love such things we fall away from truth, and cannot discover what they imitate, and so we pant for them as if they were the prime objects of beauty. Getting further away from these primal objects we embrace our phantasms. When we return to seek truth phantasms meet us in the way and will not allow us to pass on, attacking us like brigands, not indeed with violence but with dangerous pitfalls, because we do not know how widely applicable is the saying: "Keep yourselves from images" (I John 5:21).

96. So some go vaguely wandering in thought through innumerable worlds. Others have thought that God cannot exist except as

corporeal fire. Others have thought of God as
the brightness of an immense light radiating
through infinite space in all directions, except
that on one side it is cloven as by a black
wedge. They are of opinion that there are two
realms, one over against the other, and they set
up two opposing principles as fabulous as their
phantasms. If I were to urge them to declare
on oath whether they know that these things
are true, probably they would not dare to go
so far; but they might reply: *You* show us
what truth is. If I were to reply simply that
they should look for the light that enables them
to be certain that believing is one thing and
knowing another, they themselves would
swear that that light cannot be seen with the
eyes, nor thought of as filling any space however vast, and yet that it is everywhere present
to those who seek; and that nothing can be
found more certain or more serene.

97. All that I have said about the light of
the mind is made clear by that same light.
By it I know that what I have said is true, and
that I know that I know it. I know that that
light has extension neither in space nor in time.
I know that I cannot know unless I am alive,
and I know more certainly that by knowing I
attain a richer life. Eternal life surpasses temporal life in vivacity, and only by knowing do
I get a glimpse of what eternity is. By looking
at eternity with the mind's eye I remove from
it all changeableness, and in eternity I see no

temporal duration, for periods of time are constituted by the movements, past or future, of things. In eternity there is neither past nor future. What is past has ceased to be, and what is future has not yet begun to be. Eternity is ever the same. It never "was" in the sense that it is not now, and it never "will be" in the sense that it is not yet. Wherefore, eternity alone could have said to the human mind "I am what I am." And of eternity alone could it be truly said: "He who is hath sent me" (Ex. 3:14).

l, 98. If we cannot yet cleave to eternity, at least let us drive away our phantasms, and cast out of our mental vision trifling and deceptive games. Let us use the steps which divine providence has deigned to make for us. When we delighted over much in silly figments, and grew vain in our thoughts, and turned our whole life into vain dreams, the ineffable mercy of God did not disdain to use rational angelic creatures to teach us by means of sounds and letters, by fire and smoke and cloudy pillar, as by visible words. So with parables and similitudes in a fashion he played with us when we were children, and sought to heal our inward eyes by smearing them with clay.

99. Let us then make clear to ourselves what faith we ought to repose in history and what in intelligence; what we ought to commit to memory, not knowing that it is true but believing all the same; where is the truth

that neither comes nor passes away but abides
ever the same; what is the mode of interpreting
allegory, believed to have been spoken in wisdom through the Holy Spirit; whether it is
enough to allegorize things that have been
seen in ancient days and in more recent times,
or is it to be applied to the affections and nature of the soul, and to unchangeable eternity.
Do some stories signify visible deeds, others
movements of minds, and others the law of
eternity; or are some found in which all these
are to be discovered? What is stable faith, historical and temporal or spiritual and eternal,
according to which all interpretation of au-
thoritative writings is to be directed? What
advantage is to be derived from believing temporal things for knowing and possessing eternal things, which is the end of all good actions?
What is the difference between allegorizing
history and allegorizing facts or speeches or
sacraments? How is the diction of the divine
Scriptures to be received according to the
idiom of various languages? Every language
has its own special modes of expression which
seem absurd when translated into another
language. What is the advantage of such a
lowly form of speech? For in the sacred books
we find mention made of the anger of God, his
sadness, his awaking from sleep, his remember-
ing and forgetting, and other things which can
happen to good men. Not only so, there is also
mention of his repentance, his zeal, his feasting

and other such things. Are God's eyes and hands and feet, and other members named in Scripture, to be held to refer to something like the visible form of the human body? Or do they signify intelligible and spiritual powers, as do such words in Scripture as helmet, shield, sword, girdle and the like? Above all we must ask how it profits the human race that the divine providence has spoken to us by human rational and corporeal creatures who have been the servants of God. When we have come to know that one truth, all puerile impudence is driven from our minds and holy religion comes into its own.

li, 100. Putting aside, therefore, all theatrical and poetic trifling, let us by the diligent study of the divine Scriptures, find food and drink for our minds; for they are weary and parched with the hunger and thirst of vain curiosity, and desire in vain to be refreshed and satisfied with silly phantasms, as unreal as painted banquets. Let us be wholesomely educated by this truly liberal and noble game. If wonderful and beautiful spectacles afford us delight, let us desire to see wisdom "which teaches from one end to the other with might, and pleasantly disposes of all things." What is more wonderful than incorporeal might making and ruling the corporeal world? What more beautiful than its ordering and adorning the material world?

lii, 101. All admit that these things are perceived by the body, and that the mind is better than the body. Will not the mind by itself have some object that it can perceive which must be far more excellent and far nobler? We are put in mind by the things of which we are judges to look to that standard by which we judge. We turn from artistic works to the law of the arts, and we shall behold with the mind the form by comparison with which all the things are tarnished which its very goodness has made beautiful. "For the invisible things of God from the creation of the world are clearly seen, being understood by the things that are made, even his eternal power and Godhead" (Rom. 1:20). This is the return from temporal to eternal things, and the transformation of the old man into the new. What can fail to urge man to strive for virtue, when his very vices urge him? Curiosity seeks nothing but knowledge, which cannot be certain knowledge unless it be knowledge of eternal things which remain ever the same. Pride seeks nothing but power, which has reference to facility in acting. But power is attained only by the perfect soul which is submissive to God and which with great love turns towards his kingdom. Bodily pleasure seeks nothing but rest, and there is no rest save where there is no poverty and no corruption. We must beware of the creatures of the lower regions, i.e., of severer penalties after this life, where there can be no reminder of truth because there is no reasoning. And there is no reasoning because there is no shining of "the light that lighteth every man coming into this world" (John 1:9). Wherefore, let us hasten and walk while it is day lest darkness come upon us. Let us hasten to be set free from the second death, where no one is who is mindful of God, and where no one will make confession to God.

liii, 102. But unhappy men make light of what they have come to know, and rejoice in novelties. They take greater pleasure in learning than in knowing, though knowledge is the end of learning. They hold facility in acting to be a poor thing and prefer the battle to the victory, though victory is the end of battle. Those who care little for bodily health prefer to eat too much rather than to eat just enough for satiety. They prefer to enjoy sexual acts rather than to suffer no such agitation. Some even prefer to sleep rather than not to be drowsy. And yet the end of all these desires is *not* to be hungry or thirsty, *not* to seek intercourse with a woman, *not* to be weary.

103. Those who desire these true ends first put off curiosity; for they know that certain knowledge which is within, and they enjoy it as far as they can in this life. Then they put off obstinacy and receive facility in acting, knowing that it is a greater and easier victory not to resist the animosity of any one. And they remain of this opinion so far as they can in this life. Lastly, they seek bodily tranquillity by

abstaining from things that are not necessary for living this life. So they taste how sweet is the Lord. They have no doubt as to what will be after this life, and their perfection is nourished by faith, hope and charity. After this life, knowledge will be made perfect. For now we know in part, but when that which is perfect is come, knowledge will not be in part. There will be perfect peace, for there will be no other law in my members fighting against the law of my mind, but the grace of God through Jesus Christ our Lord will set us free from the body of this death. To a great extent we agree with the adversary while we are with him in the way. The body will be entirely whole without lack or weariness; for this corruptible will put on incorruption in its due time and order, when the resurrection of the flesh comes. There is no marvel if this is given to those who, in knowing, love truth alone, and, in action, love peace alone, and, in the body, love wholeness and nothing besides. What they most love in this life will be made perfect for them after this life.

liv, 104. To those who make a bad use of so good a thing as the mind, desiring visible things outside the mind which ought to remind them to behold and love intelligible things, to them will be given outer darkness. The beginning of this darkness is fleshly knowledge and the weakness of the bodily senses. Those who delight in strife will be aliens from peace and involved in frightful difficulties. The beginning of the greatest difficulty is war and contention. And this I suppose is signified by the fact that their hands and feet are bound, i.e., all facility of working is taken from them. Those who want to hunger and thirst, to burn with lust and be weary, so that they may have pleasure in eating and drinking, in lying with a woman, and in sleeping, love indigence which is the beginning of the greatest woes. What they love will be made perfect for them, for they will be where there is weeping and gnashing of teeth.

105. There are many who love all these vices together. Their whole life is a round of seeing spectacles, striving, eating, drinking, sleeping, having sexual intercourse. They have nothing in their thoughts but to embrace the phantasms which arise out of a life like that, and from their deceptions to set up rules of superstition or impiety to deceive themselves. To these they adhere even when they try to abstain from the enticements of the flesh. They do not make a good use of the talent committed to them, i.e., keenness of mind in which all seem to excel who are called learned, polished or elegant, but keep it bound up in a napkin or buried in the earth, i.e., wrapt up in voluptuous and superfluous things, and crushed beneath earthly cupidities. Therefore their hands and feet will be bound, and they will be sent into outer darkness where there will be weeping and gnashing of teeth. Not because

they loved these woes—for who could love
them?—but because the things they loved were
the beginnings of these woes, and necessarily
bring those who love them to this evil plight.
Those, who love the journey rather than the
return home or the journey's end, are to be
sent into distant parts. They are flesh and
spirit continually on the move and never
reaching home.

106. But he who makes a good use even of
his five bodily senses, to believe and praise the
works of God, to cultivate love of God, to
seek tranquillity of thought and action, and to
know God, *he* enters into the joy of his Lord.
The talent is taken from him who made a bad
use of it, and is given to him who made a good
use of his five talents. Not indeed that keenness of intellect can be transferred from one
to another. What is meant is that clever people
who neglect their minds and are impious can
lose their gift, and that diligent and pious people who are of a slower understanding can
nevertheless reach understanding. The talent
was not given to him who had received two
talents, for he who lives aright both in thought
and action already has all he needs. It was given
to him who had received five. For he has not
yet sufficient mental strength to contemplate
eternal things who puts his trust in visible and
temporal things. But he can acquire it who
praises God, the maker of all sensible things;

who trusts God by faith, waits on God in hope, and seeks him in love.

lv, 107. This being so, my dearly beloved friends and brethren, I exhort you as I exhort myself to run with all possible speed after that to which God calls us by his wisdom. Let us not love the world since all that is in the world is lust of the flesh, lust of the eye, and the pride of the world. Do not let us love to corrupt or be corrupted by fleshly pleasure, lest we come to a yet more miserable corruption of grief and torment. Do not let us love strife, lest we be given over to the power of the angels who rejoice in stife, to be humbled, bound and beaten. Let us not love spectacles, lest we wander from the truth and love shadows and are cast into darkness.

108. Let not our religion consist in phantasms of our own imagining. Any kind of truth is better than any fiction we may choose to produce. And yet we must not worship the soul, though the soul remains true even when we entertain false imaginations about it. Stubble, which is nevertheless real, is better than light fabricated at will by the vain thought of him who imagines it; and yet it would be madness to hold stubble, which we can perceive and touch, to be worthy of our worship. Let not our religion be the worship of human works. The workmen are better than their works, yet we must not worship them. Let not

our religion be the worship of beasts. The worst men are better than beasts, but we must not worship them. Let not our religion be the worship of dead men. If they lived pious lives, it must not be supposed that they seek divine honours. They want us to worship him, in whose light they rejoice to have us as sharers in their merit. They are to be honoured by imitation and not adored with religious rites. If they lived evil lives, wherever they now are, they are not to be worshipped. Let not our religion be the worship of demons, for all superstition is the punishment and the deadly disgrace of men, but it is the glory and triumph of demons.

109. Let not our religion be the worship of lands and waters. Air is purer and clearer than these, though it can also be foggy; we must not worship air. Let not our religion be the worship of the purer and more serene upper air, for it is dark when there is no light. Purer than air is the brightness of fire, which, however, we ought not to worship, since we can kindle and extinguish it at will. Let not our religion be the worship of ethereal and celestial bodies, for although they are rightly preferred to all other bodies, still any kind of life is better than they. If they are animated by a soul, any soul in itself is better than any animated body, and yet no one has ever thought that a vicious soul was to be worshipped. Let not our religion be the worship of the life that trees

live, for it is not sentient life. It is of the kind
that goes on in the rhythm of our bodies, the
sort of life that our bones and hair have, and
our hair can be cut without our feeling anything. Sentient life is better than this, and yet
we must not worship such life as beasts have.

110. Let not our religion be the worship of
the perfectly wise rational soul, as it is found
in angels who steadfastly carry on their min-
istry in the universe or in its parts, or in the
best of men who await the reformation of
their lower selves. All rational life obeys the
voice of unchangeable truth speaking silently
within the soul. If it does not so obey it is
vicious. Rational life therefore does not owe
its excellence to itself, but to the truth which
it willingly obeys. The lowest man must worship the same God as is worshipped by the
highest angel. In fact it is by refusing to worship him that human nature has been brought
low. The source of wisdom and of truth is the
same for angel and man, namely the one unchangeable Wisdom and Truth. The very Virtue and changeless Wisdom of God, consubstantial and coeternal with the Father, for our
salvation deigned, in the temporal dispensation, to take upon himself our nature in order
to teach us that man must worship what every
rational intellectual creature must also worship. Let us believe that the highest angels and
most excellent ministers of God want us to join
them in the worship of the one God, in con-

templation of whom they find their happiness.
Even we are not made happy by seeing an
angel but by seeing the truth, by which we
love the angels too and rejoice with them. We
do not grudge that they should have readier
access to the truth and enjoy it without obstacle. Rather we love them because we are
bidden by our common Lord to hope for the
same condition hereafter. So we honour them
with love, but not with divine worship. We do
not build temples for them. They do not wish
to be honoured by us in that way, because they
know that when we are good men we are ourselves the temples of the most high God. Accordingly it is written, with complete pro-
priety that an angel once forbade a man to
worship him, bidding him worship the one
God under whom both angel and man were
fellow-servants (Rev. 19:10).

111. Those who invite us to serve and worship themselves as gods are like proud men
who, if they could, would like to be worshipped in that way. It is less perilous to endure
such men than to worship demons. All lordship
of men over men is brought to an end by the
death of the lord or of the servant. Servitude
under the pride of the evil angels is more to
be feared on account of the time that is to follow death. Anyone can easily see that under a
human lord we are allowed to have our
thoughts free. We fear the lordship of demons
because it is exercised over the mind in which

is found our only means of beholding and grasping the truth. Wherefore, though we be enchained and subjected to all the powers given to men to rule the state, provided we "render unto Caesar the things that are Caesar's and to God the things that are God's" (Matt. 22:21), there is no need to fear lest anyone should exact such service after we are dead. The servitude of the soul is one thing, the servitude of the body quite another. Just men who have all their joy in God alone congratulate those who praise *him* for their good deeds. But when they are praised themselves, where possible they correct the erring. Where that is not possible, they are so far from being grateful for the error that they are eager to have it corrected. The good angels and all the holy ministers of God are like these, only more holy and pure. We need not fear lest we offend any of them if we avoid superstition, and with their help tend towards God alone, and bind [*religare*] our souls to him alone without superstition. Hence, it is believed, religion derives its name.

112. One God alone I worship, the sole principle of all things, and his Wisdom who makes every wise soul wise, and his Gift [*munus*] whereby all the blessed are blessed. I am certainly sure that every angel that loves this God loves me too. Whoever abides in him and can hear human prayers, hears me in him. Whoever has God as his chief good, helps me

in him, and cannot grudge my sharing in him.
Let those who adore or flatter the parts of the
world tell me this. What good friend will the
man lack who worships the one God whom
all the good love, in knowing whom they rejoice, and by having recourse to whom as their
first principle they derive their goodness?
Every angel that loves his own aberrations
and will not be subject to the truth, but desires
to find joy in his own advantage, has fallen
away from the common good of all and from
true beatitude. To such all evil men are given
to be subdued and oppressed. But no good man
is given over into his power except to be tried
and proved. None can doubt that such an angel
is not to be worshipped, for our misery is his
joy, and our return to God is his loss.

113. Let our religion bind us to the one
omnipotent God, because no creature comes
between our minds and him whom we know
to be the Father and the Truth, i.e., the inward
light whereby we know him. In him and with
him we venerate the Truth, who is in all respects like him, and who is the form of all
things that have been made by the One, and
that endeavour after unity. To spiritual minds
it is clear that all things were made by this
form which alone achieves what all things seek
after. But all things would not have been made
by the Father through the Son, nor would
they be preserved within their bounds in safety
unless God were supremely good. He

grudges nothing to any, for he has given to all
the possibility to be good, and has given to all
the power to abide in the good as far as they
would or could. Wherefore it befits us to keep
and to worship the Gift [*donum*] of God,
equally unchangeable with the Father and the
Son, in a Trinity of one substance. We worship one God from whom, through whom and
in whom we have our being, from whom we
fell away, being made unlike him, by whom
we have not been allowed to perish, the principle to which we have recourse, the form we
imitate, the grace whereby we are reconciled.
We worship one God by whom we were
made and his likeness by whom we are formed
for unity, and his peace whereby we cleave to
unity; God who spoke and it was done; and
the Word by whom all was made that has substance and nature; and the Gift of his benig-
nity by whom nothing that he made through
the Word should perish, but should please and
be reconciled to its Creator; one God by
whose creative work we live, by whom we are
remade so that we may live in wisdom, and by
loving and enjoying whom we live in blessedness; one God from whom, through whom,
and in whom are all things. To him be glory
for ever and ever. Amen.